Exam Ref PL-900
Microsoft Power
Platform Fundamentals

Second Edition

Craig Zacker

Exam Ref PL-900 Microsoft Power Platform Fundamentals, Second Edition

Published with the authorization of Microsoft Corporation by:
Pearson Education, Inc.

ISBN-13: 978-0-13-795658-6
ISBN-10: 0-13-795658-4

Library of Congress Control Number: 2023932829

1 2023

TRADEMARKS

Microsoft and the trademarks listed at http://www.microsoft.com on the "Trademarks" webpage are trademarks of the Microsoft group of companies. All other marks are property of their respective owners.

WARNING AND DISCLAIMER

Every effort has been made to make this book as complete and as accurate as possible, but no warranty or fitness is implied. The information provided is on an "as is" basis. The author, the publisher, and Microsoft Corporation shall have neither liability nor responsibility to any person or entity with respect to any loss or damages arising from the information contained in this book or from the use of the programs accompanying it.

SPECIAL SALES

For information about buying this title in bulk quantities, or for special sales opportunities (which may include electronic versions; custom cover designs; and content particular to your business, training goals, marketing focus, or branding interests), please contact our corporate sales department at corpsales@pearsoned.com or (800) 382-3419.

For government sales inquiries, please contact governmentsales@pearsoned.com.

For questions about sales outside the U.S., please contact intlcs@pearson.com.

CREDITS

EDITOR-IN-CHIEF
Brett Bartow

EXECUTIVE EDITOR
Loretta Yates

DEVELOPMENT EDITOR
Songlin Qiu

MANAGING EDITOR
Sandra Schroeder

SENIOR PROJECT EDITOR
Tracey Croom

COPY EDITOR
Scout Festa

INDEXER
Ken Johnson

PROOFREADER
Donna E. Mulder

TECHNICAL EDITOR
Vince Averello

EDITORIAL ASSISTANT
Cindy Teeters

COVER DESIGNER
Twist Creative, Seattle

COMPOSITOR
codeMantra

Pearson's Commitment to Diversity, Equity, and Inclusion

Pearson is dedicated to creating bias-free content that reflects the diversity of all learners. We embrace the many dimensions of diversity, including but not limited to race, ethnicity, gender, socioeconomic status, ability, age, sexual orientation, and religious or political beliefs.

Education is a powerful force for equity and change in our world. It has the potential to deliver opportunities that improve lives and enable economic mobility. As we work with authors to create content for every product and service, we acknowledge our responsibility to demonstrate inclusivity and incorporate diverse scholarship so that everyone can achieve their potential through learning. As the world's leading learning company, we have a duty to help drive change and live up to our purpose to help more people create a better life for themselves and to create a better world.

Our ambition is to purposefully contribute to a world where

- Everyone has an equitable and lifelong opportunity to succeed through learning
- Our educational products and services are inclusive and represent the rich diversity of learners
- Our educational content accurately reflects the histories and experiences of the learners we serve
- Our educational content prompts deeper discussions with learners and motivates them to expand their own learning (and worldview)

While we work hard to present unbiased content, we want to hear from you about any concerns or needs with this Pearson product so that we can investigate and address them.

- Please contact us with concerns about any potential bias at https://www.pearson.com/report-bias.html.

Contents at a glance

Contents

Chapter 3   Describe the business value of Power BI   85

Chapter 4   Demonstrate the capabilities of Power Apps   143

Chapter 5   Demonstrate the capabilities of Power Automate   177

Chapter 6 Demonstrate the capabilities of Power Virtual Agents 217

About the Author

CRAIG ZACKER is the author or coauthor of dozens of books, manuals, articles, and websites on computer and networking topics. He has also been an English professor, a technical and copy editor, a network administrator, a webmaster, a corporate trainer, a technical support engineer, a minicomputer operator, a literature and philosophy student, a library clerk, a photographic darkroom technician, a shipping clerk, and a newspaper boy.

Introduction

The Microsoft Certified: Power Platform Fundamentals certification is the initial entry point into a hierarchy of Microsoft Power Platform certifications. The PL-900: Microsoft Power Platform Fundamentals exam tests the candidate's knowledge of the components and capabilities of the four Microsoft Power Platform products: Power BI, Power Apps, Power Automate, and Power Virtual Agents, without delving deeply into specific programming and administration procedures.

With the Power Platform Fundamentals certification in place, candidates can then move on to the Microsoft Certified: Power Platform App Maker Associate certification (Exam PL-100: Microsoft Power Platform App Maker) and the Microsoft Certified: Data Analyst Associate certification (Exam DA-100: Analyzing Data with Microsoft Power BI). These two are specialist certifications covering more advanced areas of the Power Apps and Power BI products, respectively.

This book covers all the skills measured by the PL-900 exam, with each of the main areas covered in a separate chapter. Each chapter is broken down into individual skill sections, which cover all the suggested topics for each skill. It is recommended that you access trial versions of the Power Platform tools as you work your way through this book. Nothing can replace actual hands-on experience, and Microsoft provides fully functional evaluation platforms of Power Platform tools, all the components of which are accessible in the cloud and require no hardware other than a computer with internet access. Microsoft also provides a wealth of documentation for all the Power Platform tools at docs.microsoft.com. With these tools, as well as some time and dedication, you can prepare yourself for the PL-900 exam and the first step toward your certification path.

Organization of this book

This book is organized by the "Skills measured" list published for the exam. The "Skills measured" list is available for each exam on the Microsoft Learn website: *http://microsoft.com/learn*. Each chapter in this book corresponds to a major topic area in the list, and the technical tasks in each topic area determine a chapter's organization. If an exam covers six major topic areas, for example, as this one does, the book will contain six chapters.

Preparing for the exam

Microsoft certification exams are a great way to build your résumé and let the world know about your level of expertise. Certification exams validate your on-the-job experience and product knowledge. Although there is no substitute for on-the-job experience, preparation through study and hands-on practice can help you prepare for the exam. This book is not designed to teach you new skills.

We recommend that you augment your exam preparation plan by using a combination of available study materials and courses. For example, you might use the Exam Ref and another study guide for your "at home" preparation and take a Microsoft Official Curriculum course for the classroom experience. Choose the combination that you think works best for you. Learn more about available classroom training and find free online courses and live events at *http://microsoft.com/learn*. Microsoft Official Practice Tests are available for many exams at *http://aka.ms/practicetests*.

Note that this Exam Ref is based on publicly available information about the exam and the author's experience. To safeguard the integrity of the exam, authors do not have access to the live exam.

Microsoft certifications

Microsoft certifications distinguish you by proving your command of a broad set of skills and experience with current Microsoft products and technologies. The exams and corresponding certifications are developed to validate your mastery of critical competencies as you design and develop, or implement and support, solutions with Microsoft products and technologies both on-premises and in the cloud. Certification brings a variety of benefits to the individual and to employers and organizations.

> **MORE INFO**   **ALL MICROSOFT CERTIFICATIONS**
>
> For information about Microsoft certifications, including a full list of available certifications, go to *http://www.microsoft.com/learn*.

Check back often to see what is new!

Quick access to online references

Throughout this book are addresses to webpages that the author has recommended you visit for more information. Some of these links can be very long and painstaking to type, so we've shortened them for you to make them easier to visit. We've also compiled them into a single list that readers of the print edition can refer to while they read.

Download the list at *MicrosoftPressStore.com/ExamRefPL900/downloads*.

The URLs are organized by chapter and heading. Every time you come across a URL in the book, find the hyperlink in the list to go directly to the webpage.

Errata, updates & book support

We've made every effort to ensure the accuracy of this book and its companion content. You can access updates to this book—in the form of a list of submitted errata and their related corrections—at:

MicrosoftPressStore.com/ExamRefPL900/errata

If you discover an error that is not already listed, please submit it to us at the same page.

For additional book support and information, please visit *MicrosoftPressStore.com/Support*.

Please note that product support for Microsoft software and hardware is not offered through the previous addresses. For help with Microsoft software or hardware, go to *support.microsoft.com*.

Stay in touch

Let's keep the conversation going! We're on Twitter: *twitter.com/MicrosoftPress*.

CHAPTER 1

Describe the business value of Microsoft Power Platform

Microsoft Power Platform is a collection of tools that are designed to simplify the process of gathering, processing, and reporting company data. Although the Power Platform tools are suitable for professional development efforts—and Microsoft uses them to build their own Dynamics 365 and Office 365 extensibility functions—they require little or no coding and are intended for use by people with no formal software development training or experience, whom Microsoft refers to as citizen developers.

The main Power Platform tools, as shown in Figure 1-1, are designed to provide users with the ability to perform three key actions on their data: analyze, act, and automate. The tools that perform these actions are as follows:

- *Power BI* (Business Intelligence)—With this data analytics service, users can discover and gather data from local and cloud sources and then visualize and share that data.

- *Power Apps*—This development platform allows users to act on their data by creating web and mobile applications without writing code.

- *Power Automate (formerly Microsoft Flow)*—Users can use this automation service to trigger complex processes and workflows.

- *Power Virtual Agents*—Users can create chatbots using a graphical interface with no coding.

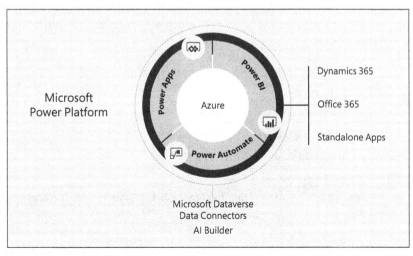

FIGURE 1-1 Microsoft Power Platform components

In addition to these components, Power Platform includes the following underlying services that work together with all the tools:

- *Microsoft Dataverse*—A cloud-based service that stores and secures data in tables, for use in any of the Power Platform services and Dynamics 365 applications.
- *Data connectors*—Proxy wrappers that enable the Power Platform tools to interact with other services. Hundreds of public connectors are available, and users can also define custom connectors.
- *AI Builder*—A turnkey solution that allows users to enhance their Power Platform apps and flows by integrating AI functions, such as object detection, text classification, and form processing.

> ***NEED MORE REVIEW?* POWER PLATFORM FUNDAMENTALS**
>
> For more information on the Power Platform components, see *https://docs.microsoft.com/en-us/learn/paths/power-plat-fundamentals*.

Skills covered in this chapter:

- Skill 1.1: Describe the business value of Microsoft Power Platform services
- Skill 1.2: Describe the business value of extending business solutions by using Microsoft Power Platform
- Skill 1.3: Describe Microsoft Power Platform administration and security

Skill 1.1: Describe the business value of Microsoft Power Platform services

The Microsoft Power Platform elements allow businesses to work with their data in more efficient ways, by analyzing and displaying it with Power BI, modifying and processing it with Power Apps, automating its collection with Power Automate, and sharing it with customers using Power Virtual Agents.

This skill covers how to:

- Gain insights into data by using Power BI
- Build applications quickly by using Power Apps
- Automate processes by using Power Automate
- Use connectors to integrate services and data
- Create powerful chatbots by using the Power Virtual Agents web app and Power Virtual Agents in Microsoft Teams

---

Gain insights into data by using Power BI

Businesses are frequently inundated with data from many sources and in many formats, often more than users can easily access, interpret, and assimilate. Data in its raw form—basically tables or lists of numbers—can be difficult for large groups to understand and use effectively. This is why it has long been a common practice for businesses to convert numerical data into charts and graphs. Users can see at a glance the relationships between values in a chart that would be much more obscure in numerical form.

An individual user can easily transform the data in a Microsoft Excel spreadsheet into a chart and share it with other users, but when the data changes, the spreadsheet and chart must be updated and redistributed. In addition, today's business environments also frequently store large amounts of data in a variety of locations and media formats, not just spreadsheets maintained by a single user.

Power BI is a tool that can access data from multiple sources, transform it into a variety of graphical formats, and publish the results in a cloud-based service that users can access from any location, using virtually any device.

Power BI allows users to access and view their data in ways that are more intuitive and convenient than traditional tables and lists of numbers. Graphs and charts can provide an immediate impression of the data's current values, as opposed to a detailed examination of the numbers that can take much more time and expertise to interpret. In addition, the Power BI user interface can allow users to interact with their data, such as by displaying additional information when they click a data point.

Power BI is a tool that consists of services, applications, and connectors that can access data from multiple sources and display it in various ways. Power BI does not manipulate or modify the data in any way. Whether a user is a designer using Power BI Desktop to model data or a consumer using the Power BI reading view to display the published data, nothing that either type of user does can possibly modify or delete the underlying data itself.

Power BI consists of two main components:

- *Power BI service*—A cloud service that provides Power BI's consumer functions by allowing users to access the content that designers have created
- *Power BI Desktop*—A Windows application that designers use to gather data; transform that data by creating dashboards, reports, and apps; and publish it to the Power BI service

Consuming Power BI content

The object of Power BI is to consolidate data from multiple sources and present it in a more visually compelling manner, using graphical elements such as charts and graphs. The Power BI service is the consumer end of the tool, which runs in the cloud and allows users to access the data published by designers. Power BI visuals are accessible from the cloud using any web browser or a mobile device, as shown in Figure 1-2.

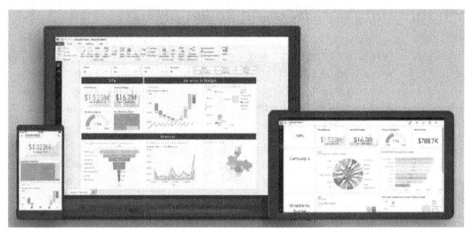

FIGURE 1-2 Visuals published in the Power BI service displayed in browsers and mobile devices

After a designer connects to a data source, creates Power BI content, and publishes it to the service, the connection to the source remains in place and the published data is updated automatically as the source data changes. Users can thus track information on a continual basis.

As with many of Microsoft's cloud-based interfaces, the Power BI service displays are composed of multiple tiles. The Power BI home page, shown in Figure 1-3, contains tiles representing the user's favorites and recently accessed elements by default, as well as a navigation menu on the left.

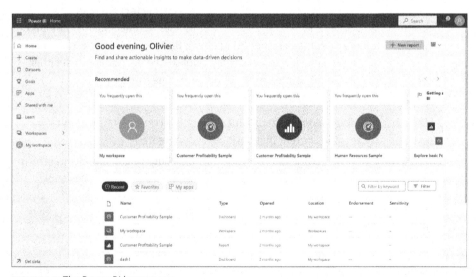

FIGURE 1-3 The Power BI home page

Using combinations of tiles, the Power BI service can display data in three basic formats: dashboards, reports, and apps, as described in the following sections.

USING DASHBOARDS

The most basic type of display in the Power BI interface is the dashboard. A dashboard (sometimes called a canvas) is a one-page view, as shown in Figure 1-4, containing tiles drawn from one or more reports that tells a single story.

FIGURE 1-4 A Power BI dashboard displaying basic human resources information for a firm

After a dashboard is published in the Power BI service, consumers can interact with it in a variety of ways. For example, clicking a tile opens the report from which the tile was taken. Hovering the cursor over an element of a graph, as shown in Figure 1-5, displays the actual data value represented.

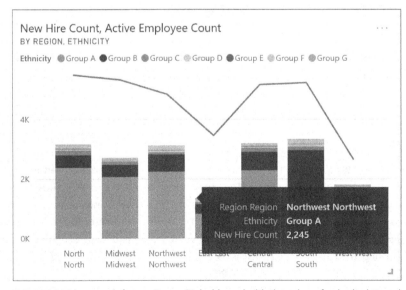

FIGURE 1-5 A bar graph from a Power BI dashboard with the value of a single data point displayed

USING REPORTS

A report is typically a multipage document that provides a more complete picture of a particular subject. By default, when a user opens a report in the Power BI interface, the main navigation pane collapses and a Pages pane appears, containing a list of the pages in the report, as shown in Figure 1-6. When you click a tile in a dashboard, the associated report opens to the page containing that tile.

FIGURE 1-6 A Power BI report containing four pages of human resources information for a firm

Reports can contain a great deal of information, so Power BI has controls that can refine the displays that appear. For example, using the Filters pane on the right allows users to configure the display to contain only data conforming to specified categories, such as dates and locations. Designers can incorporate bookmarks into reports that provide alternative views of the same data sets. Consumers can also create their own bookmarks.

USING APPS

In Power BI, an app is a collection of dashboards and/or reports that designers can package as a single content element for distribution to consumers, as shown in Figure 1-7. The advantage of app packaging for consumers is that by installing a single app, users can gain access to many dashboards and reports at once, all of which are available in one place.

> **NOTE   USING APPS**
>
> The use of apps with Power BI requires a Power BI Pro license. The basic (free) Power BI license provides users with limited consumer capabilities. The (subscription-based) Power BI Pro license, in addition to supporting apps, provides other capabilities as well, such as allowing users to share dashboards and subscribe to dashboards and reports. The Power BI Premium license is intended for large organizations and provides dedicated service capacity and huge amounts of storage. As of this writing, the Power BI Pro license is US $9.99 per month and the Power BI Premium license is US $20 per month per user and US $4,995 per month for an entire organization.

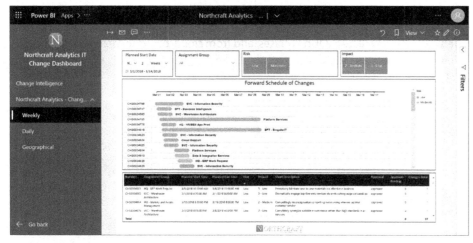

FIGURE 1-7 A Power BI app containing multiple reports

Using Power BI Desktop

Power BI Desktop is a free Windows application that designers use to create Power BI content, which will be published on the Power BI Service for consumers to use. With an interface similar to that of a Microsoft Office application, as shown in Figure 1-8, the application allows designers to create and publish data visualizations by completing tasks such as the following:

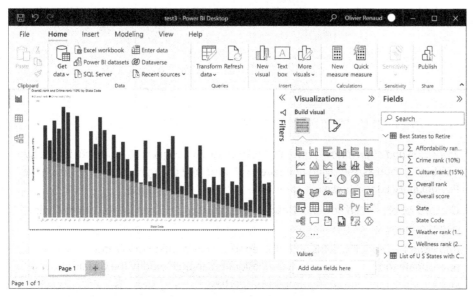

FIGURE 1-8 The Power BI Desktop interface

- *Connect to data*—Power BI Desktop provides access to hundreds of data sources, as shown in Figure 1-9, which allow designers to obtain data from the local computer, from network services such as SQL databases, and from cloud-based services such as Share-Point and Google Analytics.

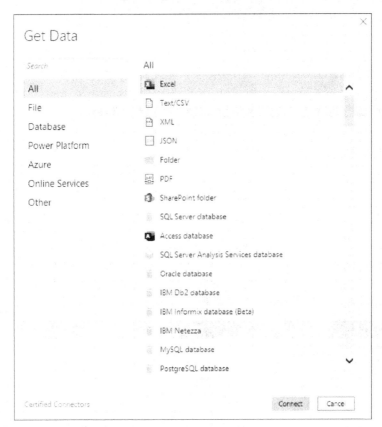

FIGURE 1-9 The Get Data dialog box in Power BI Desktop

- *Transform and clean data*—Power BI Desktop allows designers to model their data by combining sources, removing unneeded columns, and changing data types, using the Power Query Editor shown in Figure 1-10.
- *Create a report*—With Power BI Desktop, designers can create reports with multiple pages or single-page dashboards.
- *Add visuals*—Dragging fields onto the report canvas creates visualizations using an appropriate format for the data type. Designers can then modify the visualization by changing the type and configuring its properties.
- *Publish report to the Power BI service*—After the report is completed, designers can publish it to their Power BI services by selecting a specific location using the Publish to Power BI dialog box, as shown in Figure 1-11.

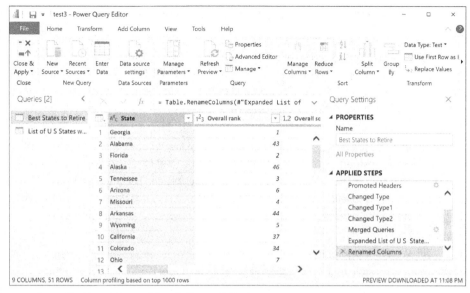

FIGURE 1-10 The Power Query Editor in Power BI Desktop

FIGURE 1-11 The Publish to Power BI dialog box in Power BI Desktop

NEED MORE REVIEW? **POWER BI INTRODUCTION**

For more information on the basics of Power BI, see *https://docs.microsoft.com/en-us/learn/modules/introduction-power-bi.*

Build applications quickly by using Power Apps

Power Apps is a collection of apps and services that work with data connectors and data sources to provide a development environment that allows Power Platform users to create their own custom business apps without requiring any coding skills. The data used by the apps can be stored in the Microsoft Dataverse that is part of the Power Platform product or in any of the more than 200 external data sources supported by the connectors included in Power Platform.

Power Apps allows businesses to automate processes that would otherwise be performed on paper. For example, instead of carrying clipboards into the field to document new information or share existing content with colleagues and clients, people can use a tablet or smartphone to record data and save it directly to a database or to display live data from a company source. Apps created with Power Apps can run on any web browser or almost any mobile device using a Power Apps app for Android or iOS.

While Power Apps is designed to be a simplified application development environment, it also provides an extensible platform that professional developers can use to create more elaborate code-based apps.

Power Apps supports the creation of three types of apps, as follows:

- *Canvas*—Apps using a development paradigm in which users start with a blank canvas, drag and drop visual elements onto it, and manipulate data using functions like those in Excel. Canvas apps provide developers with complete freedom over the design of the interface.

- *Model-driven*—Apps based on an existing model with a metadata-based architecture, which users customize by connecting to their own data sources and by selecting and configuring components, as shown in Figure 1-12. After the designer selects and models the data, Power Apps generates a user interface that is appropriate for the content.

- *Portal*—Apps realized as external facing websites created using selected pages, layouts, and content, which allow users outside of the organization to authenticate and then browse and view company data. Developers can save website projects as templates, which they can use to create new sites.

As an example, the configuration page for the sample Cost Estimator app shown in Figure 1-13 allows the designer to select any element in the app (in the left pane) and configure its appearance (in the right pane). The designer can also select the data source for the information displayed on the app page.

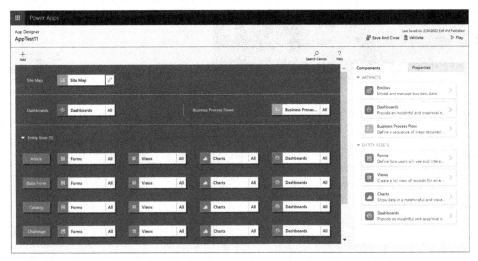

FIGURE 1-12 App Designer in Power Apps

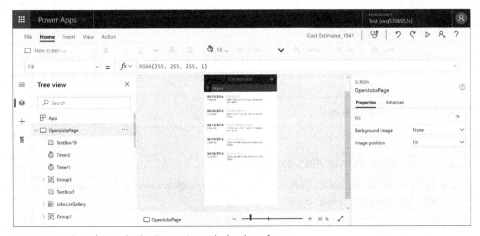

FIGURE 1-13 Sample app in the Power Apps design interface

An app can have multiple pages, each of which the designer can configure separately. In this example, shown in Figure 1-14, the app is designed for display on a smartphone-sized screen, but other form factors are available.

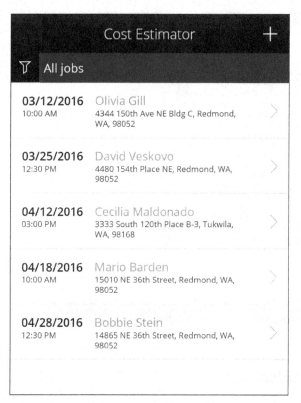

FIGURE 1-14 A Power Apps sample app

NEED MORE REVIEW? **POWER APPS INTRODUCTION**

For more information on the basics of Power Apps, see *https://docs.microsoft.com/en-us/ learn/modules/introduction-power-apps.*

Build solutions that use the Microsoft Dataverse

As noted earlier, Power Platform tools, such as Power BI and Power Apps, can access hundreds of different data sources using the connectors supplied with the product, including local sources, such as Excel workbooks; network sources, such as database servers; and cloud-based sources, such as Microsoft SharePoint Online. After a user establishes a connection to one of these data sources, the connection remains in force as long as the source remains available.

The Microsoft Dataverse is an underlying data storage solution included in Power Platform and hosted in the cloud by Microsoft Azure. The Dataverse can function as an alternative to these outside sources by furnishing data to any of the Power Platform tools, as shown in Figure 1-15. The Microsoft Dataverse is also the default data store for Dynamics 365 applications, such as Dynamics 365 Sales and Dynamics 365 Customer Service.

Microsoft Power Platform

The low code platform that spans Microsoft 365, Azure, Dynamics 365, and standalone apps.

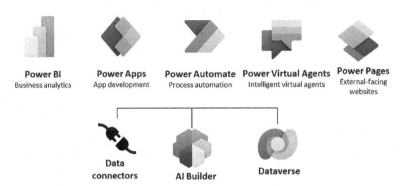

Power BI	**Power Apps**	**Power Automate**	**Power Virtual Agents**	**Power Pages**
Business analytics	App development	Process automation	Intelligent virtual agents	External-facing websites

Data connectors **AI Builder** **Dataverse**

FIGURE 1-15 Underlying services to the Power Platform tools

The Microsoft Dataverse stores data using tables, which are schemas designed to contain specific types of data. Tables consist of columns, which contain specific types of data values. The Microsoft Dataverse includes a large collection of standard tables for frequently used data types, a few of which are shown in Figure 1-16.

The tables provided in the Microsoft Dataverse are based on an open standard called the Common Data Model that Microsoft has published as part of its Open Data Initiative, developed in partnership with Adobe and SAP. The model consists of predefined tables, such as application/app, business unit, environment, region, solution, tenant, and user, each of which have columns, relationships, and metadata. Designers can also create custom tables that are specific to the data types required by a particular organization.

FIGURE 1-16 Partial listing of tables in the Microsoft Dataverse

It is common for users of Power Platform tools to access data from multiple sources and consolidate the data into a single report, app, or flow. As an alternative to maintaining multiple data source connections, it is possible to integrate the data from the sources into the Microsoft Dataverse, which can then function as a single storehouse for all the necessary local, network, or cloud data, as well as the organization's Dynamics 365 data. Users can import data from sources as a one-time event or configure the Microsoft Dataverse to synchronize with the outside data sources at scheduled intervals, ensuring that the information in the Dataverse is always current.

The Microsoft Dataverse also includes a flexible, role-based security system that administrators can use to authorize users with any degree of access they require.

Automate processes by using Power Automate

Power Automate is a tool designed to automate processes involving multiple applications that users must otherwise complete manually. Formerly called Microsoft Flow, Power Automate works by creating sequences of events that are called flows. A flow typically consists of an event (or trigger) that causes the flow processing to begin and one or more actions that the flow performs as a result of the event.

The primary advantage of Power Automate is that a flow's events and actions can involve different applications or services. For example, a user can create a flow that causes Power Automate to send a text message to the user's smartphone when the user receives an email from a specific person.

Many applications include automation capabilities within their own functions, but they typically cannot automate an action between two or more applications. Power Automate supports hundreds of connectors, triggers, and actions for different applications and services, allowing it to perform complex action sequences that would normally require manual execution. Multistep flows can incorporate actions for different applications, as shown in Figure 1-17.

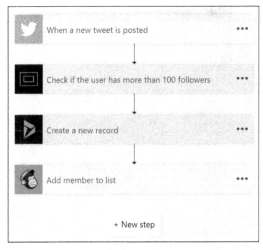

FIGURE 1-17 Events and actions of a multistep flow

The Power Automate portal includes a large selection of flow templates, as shown in Figure 1-18, which can execute common tasks or serve as the starting point for customized flows.

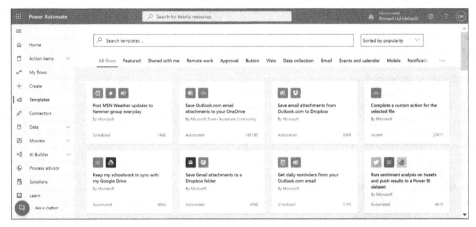

FIGURE 1-18 Flow templates in the Power Automate portal

Power Automate supports various types of flows, which you can create from the Power Automate portal or its mobile app, as shown in Figure 1-19.

FIGURE 1-19 Creating flows in the Power Automate portal

The various flow types supported by Power Automate include the following:

- *Automated cloud flows*—Perform actions without prompting when they are triggered by an event in a specific Microsoft application, such as Outlook, SharePoint, Teams, Dynamics 365, or OneDrive; a third-party application, such as Adobe Creative Cloud; or a social media site, such as Twitter.

- *Instant cloud flows* (also called button flows)—Perform specific actions when they are triggered manually by a user clicking a button or other control in the Power Automate portal or the Power Automate mobile app, as shown in Figure 1-20.

- *Scheduled cloud flows*—Perform specific actions at a specified date and time or on a recurring schedule, as configured using an interface like that shown in Figure 1-21.

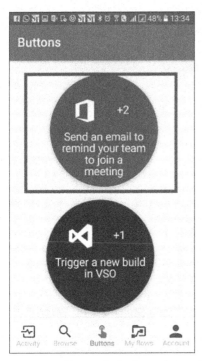

FIGURE 1-20 Buttons in the Power Automate mobile app

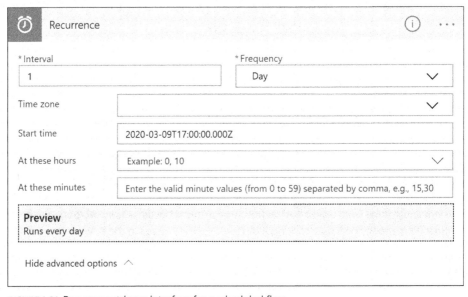

FIGURE 1-21 Recurrence trigger interface for a scheduled flow

- *Desktop flows*—Allow users to automate desktop processes by using a Power Automate Desktop app to drag and drop actions into a workspace or record and replay task sequences.
- *Business process flows*—Lead users through a prescribed process to complete a task that consists of multiple stages, each of which has multiple steps, as shown in Figure 1-22.

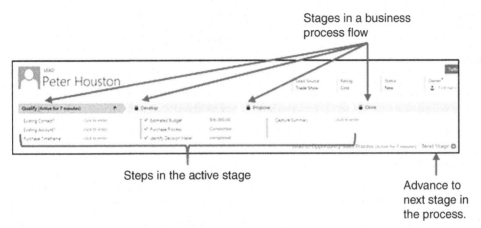

FIGURE 1-22 Stages and steps of a business process flow

Power Automate is a no-code (or low-code) tool. The interfaces for creating flows provided in the Power Automate portal and in the mobile app are graphical, which means users select input from drop-down lists or by using text boxes. However, Power Automate internally converts flows into code, as shown in Figure 1-23, and users who are so inclined can choose to work with the code directly instead of using the graphical controls.

```
1  {
2      "inputs": {
3          "host": {
4              "connectionName": "shared_sendmail",
5              "operationId": "SendEmail",
6              "apiId":
   "/providers/Microsoft.PowerApps/apis/shared_sendmail"
7          },
8          "parameters": {
9              "request/to": "Oliver__Cox@0livercox.onmicrosoft.com;",
10             "request/subject": "[Daily Reminder from Microsoft Flow]
   ",
11             "request/text": "Wake up!",
12             "request/ishtml": false
13         },
14         "authentication": "@parameters('$authentication')"
15     }
```

Done

FIGURE 1-23 Code view of a Power Automate flow

NEED MORE REVIEW? **POWER AUTOMATE INTRODUCTION**

For more information on the basics of Power Automate, see *https://docs.microsoft.com/en-us/learn/modules/introduction-power-automate*.

Use connectors to integrate services and data

All of the Power Platform tools depend on outside systems for the data they display or process. Those outside systems can be local applications, network servers, or cloud-based services. Power Platform includes hundreds of connectors, which allow the tools to access these outside resources. Wherever the data is located, the user working with the Power Platform tools must have the permissions needed to access the data. In some cases, connector configuration can call for careful management of privileges.

Power BI interoperation

Power BI accesses data on outside systems in order to display it in a different form. Designers of Power BI reports, dashboards, and apps must have the privileges needed to access the required data sources. However, the consumers of published Power BI content have no direct access to those data sources. They can only view the reports, dashboards, and apps themselves, as well as work with them by leaving comments. Consumers cannot modify reports, dashboards, and apps in other ways, such as by modifying their appearance.

There is no way for a Power BI designer or consumer to modify the original data when creating Power BI content or working with the published content. The designer is left with the sole responsibility of determining what data consumers are permitted to view. Power BI includes controls that allow the designer to share the content they create with selected users, who are permitted to view the content they create. Designers can also create workspaces that allow users to function as co-designers of Power BI content.

Power Apps and Power Automate interoperation

Power Apps and Power Automate are both tools that work bidirectionally with data sources, meaning that it is possible for an app or a flow to add or modify source data, as well as read and display it. This complicates the process of accessing and using data sources.

Power Apps and Power Automate both use connectors to access external applications, services, and data sources. Power Platform includes over 300 public connectors, a few of which are shown in Figure 1-24.

A *connector* is a proxy wrapper that the tools use to access an API provided by an application or service. Most applications and cloud services include such APIs, and the Power Platform connectors function as proxies—that is, intermediaries between the outside APIs and the internal Power Platform tools. The connector, as a proxy, authenticates to the outside application or service and then provides access to Power Apps and Power Automate (as well as to Azure Logic Apps).

FIGURE 1-24 Some of the connectors available in Power Automate

Each Power Platform connector includes a set of triggers and actions, which are specific operations that designers can use in their apps and flows. Triggers are notifications generated by the outside application or service, indicating that a specific event has occurred. For example, the creation of a new item in a certain SharePoint site can activate a trigger in the Power Platform connector for SharePoint, thereby launching a particular flow containing that trigger. There are two types of triggers in Power Platform connectors:

- *Polling triggers*—Check with the outside application or service at regular intervals for new data
- *Push triggers*—Listen for an event to occur in an outside application or service

Actions are specific changes made to an outside application or service, usually as a result of a trigger. For example, when a trigger in a Power Automate flow indicates that a new item has been created in a specific SharePoint site, the associated actions in the flow can generate notifications and send them to users by email or text message. Apps and flows can include multiple actions using different connectors, as shown in Figure 1-25.

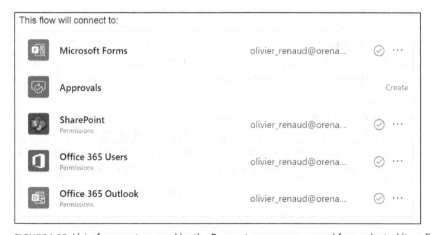

FIGURE 1-25 List of connectors used by the Request manager approval for a selected item flow template

Create powerful chatbots by using the Power Virtual Agents web app and Power Virtual Agents in Microsoft Teams

Power Virtual Agents is a recent addition to the Power Platform toolkit that allows citizen developers to create customer service chatbots and embed them into websites or Microsoft Teams pages using a simplified no-code interface. Chatbots, in this instance, are automated, text-based communication interfaces that use branching logic and artificial intelligence to communicate with online clients, ascertain their needs, and in some cases satisfy those needs by triggering flows that perform specific tasks.

When a developer creates a virtual agent and adds a default greeting, an authoring canvas, like the one shown in Figure 1-26, appears. By default, the bot's standard Greeting topic is configured to respond to any one of 52 trigger phrases representing possible initial statements by the client with a standard greeting.

FIGURE 1-26 The Power Virtual Agents default greeting

The trigger phrases do not have to match the user's input exactly. Power Virtual Agents uses a natural language understanding module to match variants of the trigger phrases with an appropriate response. The developer can add more trigger phrases and modify the bot's greeting as needed.

To extend the conversation, the developer can create additional topics that ask the user questions, obtain information from the user, and take action based on that information. For example, Figure 1-27 shows a simple yes or no question and the branching logic that allows the developer to continue the conversation in different ways, depending on the response given.

Power Virtual Agents can work together with Power Automate, so developers can create flows that perform tasks using information gathered from the user and integrate them into conversations. For example, in the case of a user wanting to check the status of an order, a topic in the bot's conversation can prompt the user to specify an order number. Then the bot can pass the order number to a flow that performs a database lookup and supplies information about the order back to the bot, which displays it to the user. For conversations that are unable to provide what the user needs, a topic can pass the user to a live agent.

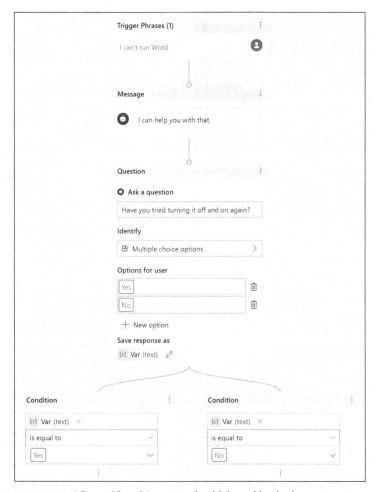

FIGURE 1-27 A Power Virtual Agents topic with branching logic

It is also possible to add Power Virtual Agents as an app in Microsoft Teams, as shown in Figure 1-28. This enables users to create chatbots for Teams users that address Teams-specific issues. After adding and launching the Power Virtual Agents app, a user creates a new chatbot by selecting the team that will be its audience.

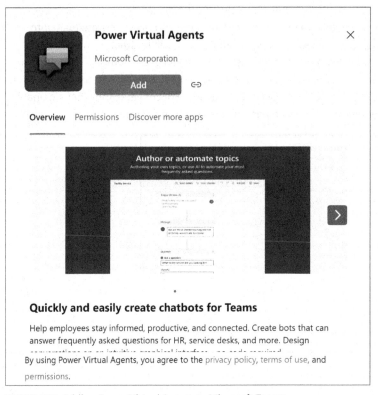

FIGURE 1-28 Adding Power Virtual Agents to Microsoft Teams

Once Power Virtual Agents creates the chatbot, as shown in Figure 1-29, the interface for creating the bot's conversation is roughly the same as that in the Power Virtual Agents portal.

FIGURE 1-29 A Power Virtual Agents chatbot in Microsoft Teams

Skill 1.2: Describe the business value of extending business solutions by using Microsoft Power Platform

Power Platform provides a layer of connectivity for a large number of business environments by allowing users to analyze their existing data, create apps that process their data, and automate their data gathering and updating processes. As an underlying collection of tools, Power Platform can provide additional connectivity both within and among the various applications and services in Dynamics 365, Microsoft 365, Microsoft Azure, and other third-party products.

This skill covers how to:
- Describe how Microsoft Power Platform apps work together with Dynamics 365 apps
- Describe how Microsoft Power Platform business solutions work together with Microsoft 365 apps and services
- Describe how Microsoft Power Platform apps work together
- Describe how to use Microsoft Power Platform solutions with Microsoft Teams
- Describe how Microsoft Power Platform business solutions can consume Microsoft Azure services including Azure Cognitive Services
- Describe how Microsoft Power Platform business solutions can consume third-party apps and services
- Describe use cases for AppSource

Describe how Microsoft Power Platform apps work together with Dynamics 365 apps

Dynamics 365 is a series of business applications that is intended to digitally transform organizations by utilizing the data that can be generated by nearly every process essential to productivity. The traditional application model of "forms over data" creates new data as a result of business transactions, whether they are customer relationship interactions or internal resource management exchanges. The interaction comes first, and data is generated as a result of workers filling out digital forms to document the activity.

Digital transformation is a reversal of this process in which the data comes first, data that is now produced by virtually every device and business process. Modern business devices, applications, and services of almost every kind are capable of generating data during their operations and can export it for processing. Virtually all business tools—from environmental devices such as thermostats and HVAC systems, to industrial machinery, to customer relationship management (CRM) and enterprise resource management (ERP) systems—are capable of generating a continuous stream of data as they operate. The Dynamics 365 applications—in cooperation with the underlying Power Platform tools—can then use this data to track performance and anticipate future incidents and conditions, thus changing a reactive system to a proactive one.

For example, in the past, a customer experiencing a vital equipment failure would have to call the manufacturer of the equipment and request a service call. The manufacturer's customer service representative would then create a service request by filling out a form in an application. Only at this point did data begin to be created. The manufacturer's support team would then start the process by which the service request's urgency was assessed, the problem investigated, and a service technician dispatched to address the problem. All during this process, the equipment was down and the customer was experiencing lost productivity.

Now, after the digital transformation, the customer's equipment can generate a constant stream of data that is relayed directly to the manufacturer. By monitoring and processing the data, the manufacturer can detect a potential problem before it causes a failure and dispatch a technician on a maintenance call.

The Dynamics 365 applications and the Power Platform tools provide the analytics needed to utilize this generated data to connect all aspects of the organization, including the human elements (employees and customers) and the business elements (products and operations). This process by which business activities generate data and the Dynamics 365 applications use that data to facilitate further business activities, as shown in Figure 1-30, is called the digital feedback loop, in Microsoft parlance.

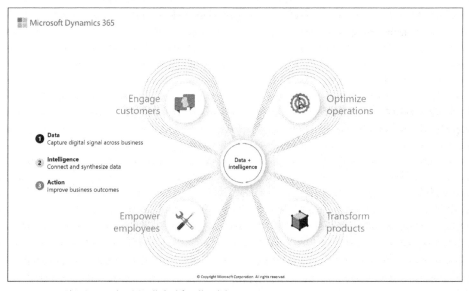

FIGURE 1-30 The Dynamics 365 digital feedback loop

Dynamics 365 is a collection of applications that all share the same data and intelligence. Here are some of the applications:

- *Sales*—Tracks customer accounts and contacts and performs marketing-related tasks

- *Customer Service*—Manages customer relationships
- *Field Service*—Provides scheduling and workflow automation for onsite mobile field workers
- *Marketing*—Works with the Sales application to create compelling documents and emails and shares marketing and sales information with internal product teams
- *Commerce*—Provides comprehensive and unified digital, call center, back-office, and in-store experiences
- *Finance*—Provides real-time performance monitoring and uses artificial intelligence to predict future financial performance
- *Human Resources*—Provides employee recordkeeping functions and tracks company-wide statistics on employee retention, training, and performance
- *Supply Chain Management*—Manages planning, inventory, and production and uses artificial intelligence to predict future needs
- *Business Central*—Provides smaller businesses with automation of sales, finance, manu-facturing, and other business processes

Microsoft originally designed the Microsoft Dataverse (formerly called the Common Data Service) as a platform for the Dynamics 365 applications, which use it to store and retrieve their data. Later, Microsoft created the Power Platform tools to function as a low-code/no-code extensibility platform for Dynamics 365 by having it use the same Dataverse. The data gener-ated by the Dynamics 365 applications is available to all the Power Platform tools, as well as to other applications and services that store data in the Microsoft Dataverse.

Describe how Power Platform business solutions work together with Microsoft 365 apps and services

Microsoft 365 is a suite of applications that includes Windows 10, Office 365, and Enterprise Mobility + Security. Power Apps and Power Automate are included with all of the Microsoft 365 products, but only the Microsoft 365 Enterprise E5 product includes the Pro version of Power BI. However, all the Power Platform tools are available as separate products and can be added to a Microsoft 365 deployment.

EXAM TIP

The original version of Power BI for Office 365 was an add-on product that added visual functionality to existing Excel Power View reports. There was also a Windows 8 app that allowed users to access those reports remotely. This version of Power BI was deprecated as of December 31, 2015, in favor of the new service-based version of Power BI that is part of the Power Platform today. When preparing for the PL-900 exam, be aware that some out-dated documentation still exists on the internet that refers to this original Power BI version and not the current one.

As noted earlier, when Microsoft began rolling out the Power Platform tools several years ago, they designed them primarily as an extensibility platform for the Dynamics 365 ERP and CRM applications. This was an obvious direction to take because the Power Platform and Dynamics 365 products were all designed to use the Microsoft Dataverse. However, Microsoft has announced their intention to expand that extensibility platform to include Microsoft 365 applications and services as well.

Unlike Dynamics 365, the Microsoft 365 components are not built on the Microsoft Dataverse, so they do not have the same shared data connection with the Power Platform tools. However, the Power Platform tools include connectors that allow them to access and use the data generated by the Microsoft 365 applications and services.

For example, citizen developers at an organization running Microsoft 365 can use Power BI to gather data from branch sites and mobile SharePoint, Exchange, and Teams users as they roam around the facilities or work in the field. The developers can then create dashboards or reports to display a conglomerated picture of the data from those various sources. Power BI allows the organization to monitor, analyze, and visualize trends in sales, supply, and other aspects of the business, helping them to anticipate needs before they arise.

Using Power Apps and AI Builder, developers can create applications that use text and image recognition to collect additional data from users as they work with Microsoft 365 applications and services, rather than requiring them to enter data manually on forms-based interfaces. For example, mobile users can photograph shelves in stores and warehouses; an app can then scan the photographs, count the number of products on the shelves, and use the data to update a Power BI dashboard with up-to-the-minute inventory information. This additional data can then also be stored in the Microsoft Dataverse.

With Power Automate, citizen developers can create flows that perform time-consuming tasks automatically. In the previous example, the automated shelf-counting app can result in the creation of orders for additional products. When a new order arrives at the supplier's mailbox, a flow can read the products requested and check the inventory to see whether they are available. If the products are available, the flow can trigger a shipment; if they are not, the flow can branch to a different process that classifies the products as back-ordered and notifies the requestor. Using the connectors supplied with the Power Platform tools, flows can interact with various Microsoft 365 applications and services.

Describe how Microsoft Power Platform apps work together

Microsoft developed the Power Platform tools as independent products, but they can now work together in a variety of ways. This is primarily due to the Microsoft Dataverse, which provides a common data storage solution for all of the tools and also serves as a workspace where the tools can temporarily store data as they are working on it.

Power BI, for example, can access data from multiple sources using connectors, and store the data in Microsoft Dataverse tables. Users can then access the data from the Dataverse and use it to create Power BI dashboards and reports. The connectors can update the data stored in the Dataverse at intervals, so the information displayed in the Power BI documents is always current.

Power Apps and Power Automate are designed to function together. Power Apps provides the user interface design capabilities that enable developers to control the appearance of the app, and Power Automate provides the means for the app to perform tasks.

Power Automate flows are the Power Platform components that actually do work. When a Power Apps app or a Power Virtual Agents chatbot needs to interact with a connected data source—to add, modify, or delete data, for example—it calls a Power Automate flow, which can carry data to the connected source, perform actions on the source's own data, and then carry the results of those actions back to the original app or bot.

Describe how to use Microsoft Power Platform solutions with Microsoft Teams

Developers can integrate the content they create using the Power Platform tools into various Microsoft 365 applications and services, including Microsoft Teams. For example, to insert a Power Apps app into Teams, the developer must use the App ID on the app's Details screen to identify the app to Teams. The App ID is a 128-bit globally unique identifier (GUID), notated as 32 hexadecimal digits, as shown in Figure 1-31.

In Microsoft Teams, the developer must first install the Apps Studio application, then create a Teams app. Rather than create a new app in Teams from scratch, the developer identifies the Power Apps app to be embedded by specifying its App ID in the Identification section of the App Details screen, as shown in Figure 1-32.

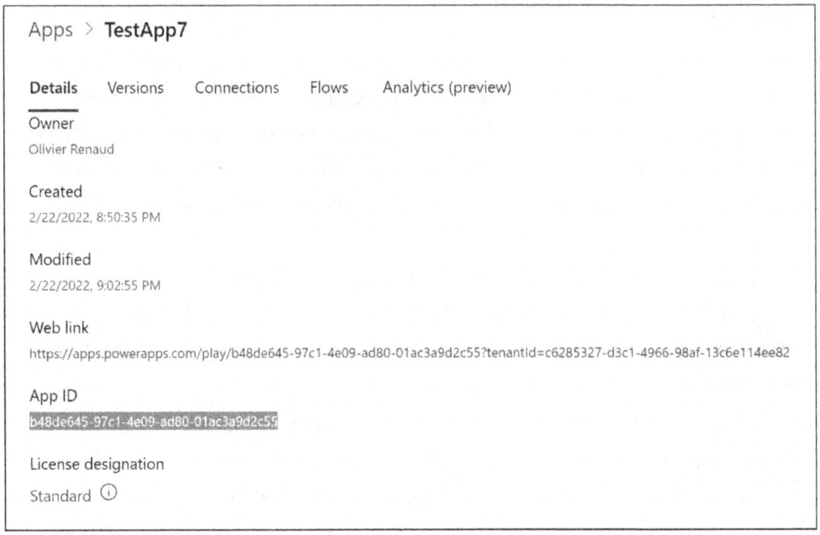

Apps > **TestApp7**

Details   Versions   Connections   Flows   Analytics (preview)

Owner
Olivier Renaud

Created
2/22/2022, 8:50:35 PM

Modified
2/22/2022, 9:02:55 PM

Web link
https://apps.powerapps.com/play/b48de645-97c1-4e09-ad80-01ac3a9d2c55?tenantId=c6285327-d3c1-4966-98af-13c6e114ee82

App ID
b48de645-97c1-4e09-ad80-01ac3a9d2c55

License designation
Standard ⓘ

FIGURE 1-31 Details screen of an app in the Power Apps portal

The developer can then complete the process of configuring the new app in Teams App Studio and distribute it to users in the tenancy. The app then appears as a tile on the Add a tab screen in Teams, enabling the developer to add it as a tab on the General screen for the selected users.

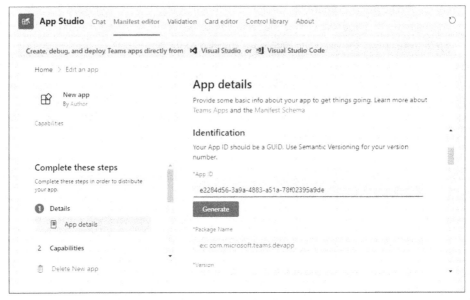

FIGURE 1-32 The App Details screen in Microsoft Teams App Studio

Describe how Microsoft Power Platform business solutions can consume Microsoft Azure services including Azure Cognitive Services

Microsoft Azure is Microsoft's cloud-based architecture for providing hundreds of Software as a Service (SaaS), Platform as a Service (PaaS), and Infrastructure as a Service (IaaS) products to customers. The Power Platform tools run on the Azure backbone and are heavily reliant on it for their cloud presence, data storage, and other resources. The Microsoft Dataverse stores its data in the Azure cloud, and the portals for the various Power Platform tools are all Azure-based cloud services.

Because it is cloud based, Microsoft Azure makes the Power Platform tools available to users at any location, using any device. Power BI, Power Apps, Power Automate, and Power Virtual Agents all have mobile apps that allow users to function as both designers and consumers using a smartphone or tablet.

In addition to providing the cloud infrastructure, Azure also hosts cloud services, some of which designers can use to enhance the capabilities of their apps and flows. For example, Azure Cognitive Services is a set of cloud-based artificial intelligence APIs that enable Power Platform users to add intelligence to apps and flows. The cognitive services Azure can provide are as follows:

- *Vision*—Enables apps to process and classify images to provide labeling and facial recognition services
- *Speech*—Provides speech-based services, including text-to-speech, speech-to-text, and speech translation

- *Language*—Provides natural language processing for interpretation and translation purposes
- *Decision*—Enables apps to monitor user content for anomalies and undesirable content

Describe how Power Platform business solutions can consume third-party apps and services

Aside from their compatibility with Microsoft applications and services, the Power Platform tools have connectors that allow them to access data sources from third-party applications and services. Hundreds of public connectors are available that allow users to work with data from various social media and other commercial products. The data sources accessed using connectors can be combined with Microsoft Dataverse data to create composite representations in Power BI, Power Apps, and Power Automate.

For applications or services with representational state transfer (REST) APIs that are not supported by the public connectors included in Power Platform, it is possible to create custom connectors. Administrators can create connectors using definition files based on the OpenAPI or Postman standard, for APIs that support them, or they can build a custom connector from scratch by creating a new definition.

Describe use cases for AppSource

AppSource is an online software store dedicated to business applications and services created and submitted by outside developers. Some of the applications have a Preferred Solution badge, indicating that they have been certified as being created by a reliable Microsoft partner.

Access to the AppSource store is integrated into the Power Platform tools as well. The Solutions page in the Power Apps portal lists the existing installed apps, but it also has an Open AppSource button, as shown in Figure 1-33.

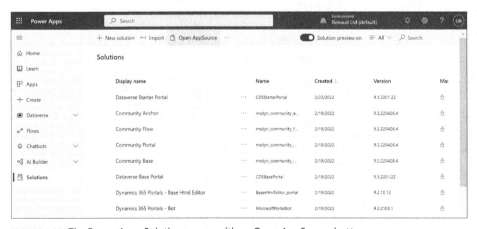

FIGURE 1-33 The Power Apps Solutions page, with an Open AppSource button

When you access the AppSource store through a Power Platform portal, a window to the store appears with a search filter already applied, limiting the display to Power Platform apps. The AppSource interface then lists the most viewed apps for Power Platform, as shown in Figure 1-34, followed by sections containing the apps for the individual Power Platform tools.

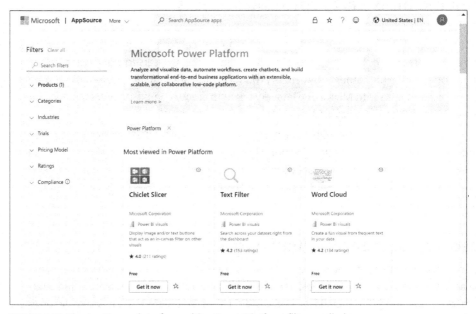

FIGURE 1-34 The AppSource interface, with a Power Platform filter applied

Skill 1.3: Describe Microsoft Power Platform administration and security

As with any other application or service, the Power Platform tools require attention to administration and security to configure them properly and prevent them from being misused.

Power Platform itself is not a single service; the name refers to a collection of services that organizations can use individually or in combination. The Power Platform tools—Power BI, Power Apps, Power Automate, and Power Virtual Agents, along with their underlying components (Microsoft Dataverse, data connectors, and AI Builder)—run as individual services, meaning that they are cloud-based software products that are hosted by Microsoft Azure on a software as a service (SaaS) basis. Each of the four main tools has its own portal, as shown in Figure 1-35, in which users can design and consume content.

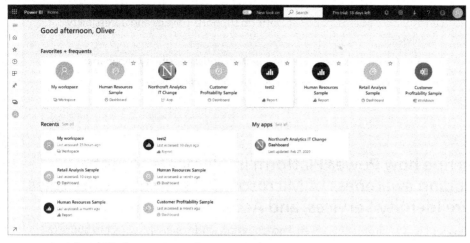

FIGURE 1-35 A Power Platform tool portal

> **NOTE POWER BI DESKTOP**
>
> The only Power Platform components that are not cloud-based services are Power BI Desktop and Power Automate Desktop. Power BI Desktop is a standalone Windows application that designers can use to establish data connections; create reports, dashboards, and apps; and upload them to the Power BI service in the cloud, which makes them available to consumers. Power BI Desktop is not an essential component; designers can create dashboards, reports, and apps in the Power BI Service portal as well. The Power Automate Desktop application enables users to automate tasks on their local computers.

Because they are Azure services, the Power Platform tools can take advantage of many of the advantages that Azure provides, including high availability due to redundant data centers, localized access using Azure Traffic Manager (ATM), and identity management provided by Azure Active Directory (AAD).

> **This skill covers how to:**
>
> - Describe how Power Platform implements security, including awareness of Microsoft Dataverse security roles, Azure Identity Services, and Access Management (IAM)
> - Describe how to manage apps and users
> - Describe environments
> - Describe where to perform specific administrative tasks, including Power Platform admin center and Microsoft 365 admin center
> - Describe data policies

- Describe how Microsoft Power Platform supports privacy and accessibility guidelines
- Describe Microsoft Power Platform privacy and accessibility capabilities
- Describe Microsoft Power Platform governance capabilities
- Describe analytics and how they can be used

Describe how Power Platform implements security, including awareness of Microsoft Dataverse security roles, Azure Identity Services, and Access Management

Any development environment—even a no-code/low-code one—is subject to abuse by unauthorized users, whether intentional or not. However, because the Power Platform tools are designed for an audience of citizen developers, as well as content consumers, security is a particularly important aspect of their administration. Code-based development environments are not understood by most users, which helps to protect them from casual interference, but they are still subject to deliberate tampering by malicious outsiders. Therefore, the Power Platform tools require security mechanisms like those of any other cloud-based service.

All of the Power Platform tools rely on Azure Active Directory, the primary element of Azure Identity Services, for user accounts and licensing. The Identity and Access Management (IAM) service enables administrators to specify the types of authentication necessary to establish a user's identity, such as multifactor authentication and single sign-on; they can also create security roles and assign them to users as needed. Administrators can also use the standard Azure tools, such as Microsoft 365 admin center, for user account maintenance and license assignment. Apart from this, the main Power Platform tools operate independently, so they each have their own security architecture. The following sections examine the security considerations for each component.

Power BI security

At its most basic, security in Power BI is a matter of sharing content with other users. Developers control access to their content by sharing dashboards, reports, or apps with specific consumers using the interface shown in Figure 1-36. However, for users to access Power BI in the first place, they must first be authenticated and authorized for specific content.

Power BI, as implemented in Microsoft Azure, is a service that consists of two clusters: the Web Front End (WFE) cluster and the Back-End cluster, as shown in Figure 1-37.

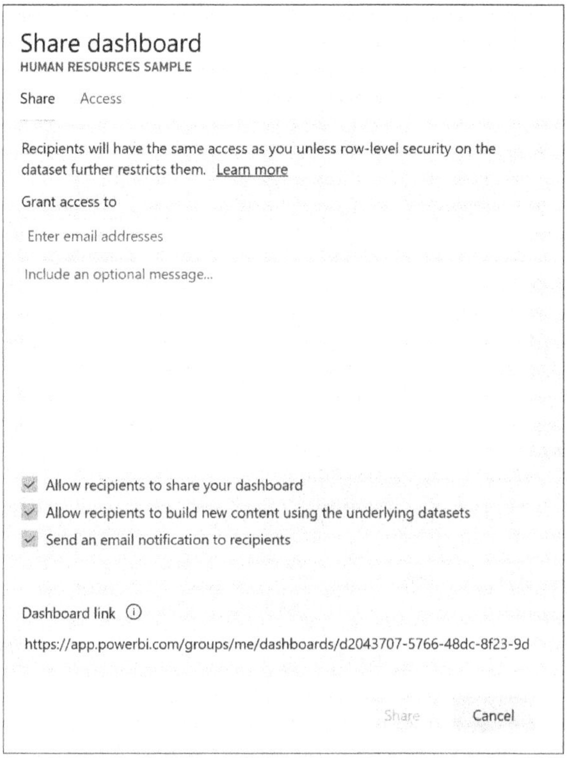

Share dashboard
HUMAN RESOURCES SAMPLE

Share   Access

Recipients will have the same access as you unless row-level security on the dataset further restricts them. Learn more

Grant access to

Enter email addresses

Include an optional message...

☑ Allow recipients to share your dashboard
☑ Allow recipients to build new content using the underlying datasets
☑ Send an email notification to recipients

Dashboard link ⓘ

https://app.powerbi.com/groups/me/dashboards/d2043707-5766-48dc-8f23-9d

Share   Cancel

FIGURE 1-36 Power BI Share Dashboard dialog box

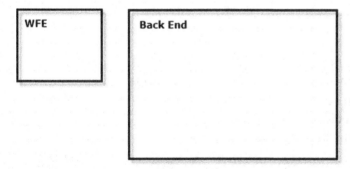

FIGURE 1-37 Power BI clusters architecture

The WFE cluster is responsible for the initial connection by users to the Power BI service and the authentication of the user account, in a process shown in Figure 1-38.

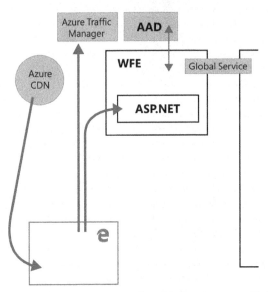

FIGURE 1-38 Browser interaction with the Power BI WFE cluster components

When a user directs a browser to Power BI by typing a URL or clicking a hyperlink, the following procedures occur:

1. The Azure Traffic Manager (ATM) examines the user's DNS record and directs the browser connection to the WFE cluster in the nearest Microsoft data center.

2. The WFE cluster directs the user connection to the Microsoft Online Services login page.

3. The user is asked to authenticate against their account in Azure Active Directory (AAD). When the authentication is successful, the login page directs the connection back to the WFE cluster.

4. The WFE cluster authorizes the user's Power BI service subscription with Azure Active Directory and, if the authorization is successful, obtains an AAD security token.

5. The WFE cluster consults the Power BI Global Service to determine the location of the correct Back-End cluster for the tenant to which the user belongs.

6. The WFE cluster directs the user connection to the correct Back-End cluster and supplies the user's browser with the AAD security token, the address of the Back-End cluster obtained from the Global Service, and information about the current session.

7. The user's browser connects to the WFE cluster and the Azure Content Delivery Network (CDN) and downloads the common files needed to interact with the Power BI service. The browser maintains these files for the duration of the session with the Power BI service.

After the authentication and authorization processes are completed successfully by the WFE cluster and the browser downloads the necessary files, all subsequent Power BI communication takes place between the browser and the Back-End cluster directly, without further participation of the WFE cluster.

The Back-End cluster hosts a variety of roles, as well as the data storage media where the Power BI information is stored, as shown in Figure 1-39. The dotted line in the figure represents the division between the modules that are accessible to users via the public internet (on the left) and those that are accessible only indirectly (on the right).

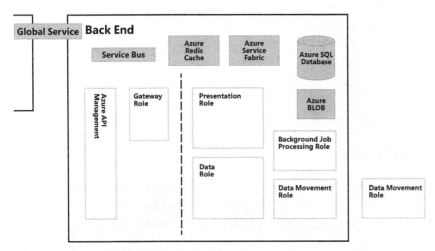

FIGURE 1-39 Power BI Back-End cluster components

The Back-End cluster is responsible for all the Power BI operations for authenticated clients, including the establishment and maintenance of data connections, the creation of the visualizations in dashboards and reports, and the storage of data. Users communicating with the Back-End cluster do so through the Gateway Role.

The Gateway Role and Azure API Management are the only modules accessible to users through the public internet. These modules accept and manage user connections, authorize users for specific content, and then relay all incoming user requests to the other modules in the cluster as needed. For example, a typical transaction in which a user attempts to access a Power BI dashboard, as shown in Figure 1-40, proceeds as follows:

1. The user's browser accesses the Power BI portal and connects to the WFE cluster.

2. The WFE cluster authenticates the user with Azure Active Directory (AAD) and authorizes the user's access to Power BI.

3. The browser connects to the Back-End cluster.

4. The user generates a request to display a dashboard and sends it to the Gateway Role in the Back-End cluster.

5. The Gateway Role forwards the request to the Presentation Role, which is responsible for supplying the data needed to create the visualization of the dashboard in the user's browser.

6. The Presentation Role sends the requested data to the Gateway Role.

7. The Gateway Role forwards the data to the user's browser, and the browser displays the requested dashboard.

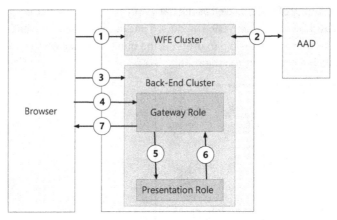

FIGURE 1-40 Power BI transaction

Thus, the Presentation Role (and all of the other non-public roles in the Back-End cluster, including the Data Role, the Background Job Processing Role, and the Data Movement Role) is protected from direct access through the internet by users, both authorized and unauthorized.

> **NOTE POWER BI PREMIUM**
>
> Power BI Premium is a subscription level that provides a tenant with a dedicated Back-End service cluster, as shown in Figure 1-41, created on virtual machines located in the same data center as the tenant.
>
> The Premium cluster contains separate instances of roles found in the Back-End cluster, including the Gateway Role, Azure API Management, Data Role, and Job Processing Role, as well as a separate Azure SQL Database. All communication with the dedicated Premium cluster goes through the shared Back-End cluster, which relays traffic to and from the Gateway Role in the Premium cluster.

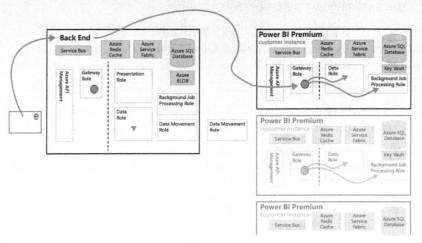

FIGURE 1-41 Power BI Premium Back-End cluster architecture

Designers should also be conscious of the security of the data they use to create dashboards and reports, in addition to the authentication needed to access the Power BI service. When Power BI designers connect to a data source, they typically have to supply credentials for a separate authentication to that source. A dashboard or report that contains the data uses the designer's credentials to access and update that data. However, when the designer shares the dashboard or report with consumers, those users are not authenticated to the original data sources. Therefore, if the data in the Power BI content is sensitive, the designer is solely responsible for making it accessible to the consumers. As noted earlier in this chapter, Power BI users cannot modify the data used to create dashboards and reports, but in situations where the data is confidential, designers must control who has access to their Power BI content.

The Back-End cluster contains two forms of data storage: Azure Blob and an Azure SQL Database instance. Azure Blob is a storage solution that Azure uses for large amounts of unstructured data. Power BI uses Azure Blob storage for data that designers import from a source, such as an Excel worksheet. Power BI uses the Azure SQL Database for all other data, including tenant information, workspaces, dashboards and reports, and metadata.

When designers access data sources, they do so in two possible ways:

- *Import*—Data accessed from a file, such as an Excel worksheet
- *DirectQuery*—Data accessed using a reference to an outside source, such as a Share-Point site or a database

The Data Role in Power BI reads imported data into an Analysis Services in-memory database, in which it is retained for up to one hour and also stored in Azure Blob storage in encrypted form. Data accessed by DirectQuery is also stored in the Analysis Services database, but only while it is *in process*—that is, when a procedure occurs that requires access to the data, such as when a user accesses a data set or modifies a report or dashboard, or when a data refresh occurs. The Analysis Services database is unencrypted to allow Power BI to access the necessary data immediately. When data is *at rest*, the opposite of *in process*, it is stored in either Azure Blob or the Azure SQL Database, and it is always encrypted.

Power Apps security

As with all the Power Platform tools, Power Apps relies on a layered security model that includes the following elements:

- *Azure Active Directory authentication*—Power Apps uses Azure Active Directory (Azure AD) user accounts to control access to its portal and to specific apps. Administrators with appropriate Azure AD credentials can assign Power Apps licenses to users and grant them access to specific apps and security roles. Administrators can also use other Azure tools to regulate access to Power Apps, including conditional access policies and the mobile application protection policies provided by Microsoft Intune.
- *Power Apps licensing*—Developers and consumers must possess a Power Apps license to access the portal, create apps, and run apps.

- *Environment security roles*—Each environment an administrator creates without a Microsoft Dataverse database in it has two built-in administrative security roles, as follows. To assign users to these roles, administrators use the interface shown in Figure 1-42, found in the Power Platform admin center. Adding the Dataverse to an environment creates many additional security roles.

  - *Environment Admin*—Can perform all administrative tasks for an environment, including adding users to the Environment Admin and Environment Maker roles, creating Microsoft Dataverse databases, and managing all other resources in the environment.

  - *Environment Maker*—Can create resources in the environment, including apps, flows, connections, custom connectors, and gateways, and share apps with other users.

FIGURE 1-42 Assigning the Environment Maker role

- *App sharing*—Developers can choose to share apps with other Azure AD users through the interface shown in Figure 1-43. By default, the selected sharers are standard users of the app, but the developer can also designate them as co-owners. A co-owner of an app can edit it and share it with others but cannot delete the app or change its owner.

- *Environment boundaries*—An *environment* is a container for apps, flows, and data that is separate from any other environments in the same tenant. A tenancy has a single environment by default, which is named for the tenant. Administrators can create all their apps and flows in that default environment, or they can choose to create additional environments in that tenant to make separate development spaces. For example, administrators can create separate environments for the various teams or departments in the organization, use them to separate testing and production versions of apps, or use them to create spaces with different security requirements. Each environment is created in a selected geographic region, and all of the environment's resources are bound to that region. If an administrator chooses to create a Microsoft Dataverse database in an environment, that database and the data it contains are only available to apps and flows created in that same environment.

- *Connector credentials*—The Share dialog box also lists the data connections used by the app. The administrator must see to it that the selected users also have credentials with the permissions required to access the data sources the app needs to function. Power Apps does not provide users with access to data for which they do not already have permissions.

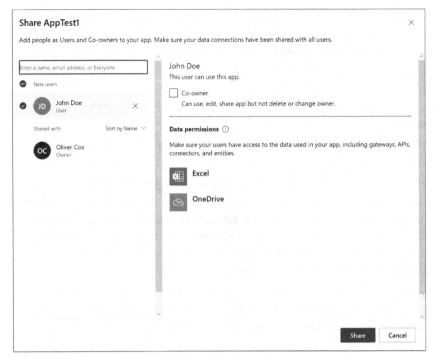

FIGURE 1-43 Power Apps Share dialog box

- *Microsoft Dataverse user security roles*—A Microsoft Dataverse database has three standard security roles, which are sets of permissions that administrators can assign to users
  and groups and which determine what operations the users can perform on database
  entities. Administrators can also create custom security roles that contain any combination of the following record-level privileges: create, read, write, delete, append, append
  to, assign, and share.

  - *System Customizer*—Provides the users with the create, read, write, and delete
    permissions for the entities they create and the permission needed to customize the
    environment.

  - *Basic User*—Allows the users to run apps in the environment and provides them with
    the read, create, write, and delete permissions for the records they own. All users
    added to the environment receive this role by default.

  - *Delegate*—Allows users to impersonate other users and run code on their behalf.

Power Automate security

When users create a flow in Power Automate (or an app in Power Apps), they must supply
authentication credentials for any connector providing access to a third-party application or
service. For example, when creating a flow that is triggered by the addition of an event to a
Google calendar, the designer must provide the credentials needed to log in to the Google
account containing the calendar to be monitored.

This fact raises a security concern that the designer must consider. Does the designer want the users with whom they share the flow or app to have access to those credentials? The answer depends on the circumstances, and designers sometimes have multiple options.

When creating and sharing canvas apps in Power Apps, designers will find that the credentials specified for some connectors are shared with the users receiving the app, whereas other connectors require the app users to specify their own credentials to gain access to a third-party application or service.

In the case of flows created with Power Automate, designers can share flows with other users in the following two ways:

- *Co-owners*—Receive full access to all the connections configured in the flow. Running the flow as is utilizes the existing connection credentials. Co-owners can also modify the flow using the existing credentials or reconfigure connections to use different credentials. However, co-owners cannot use the shared credentials to create their own new flows. Adding a co-owner to a flow causes Power Automate to display a Connections Used warning like the one shown in Figure 1-44.

- *Run-only users*—An option only in manually triggered flows. When flow creators add run-only users, they must specify whether the connections in the flow will use the credentials provided by the creator or the run-only users must specify their own credentials, as shown in Figure 1-45.

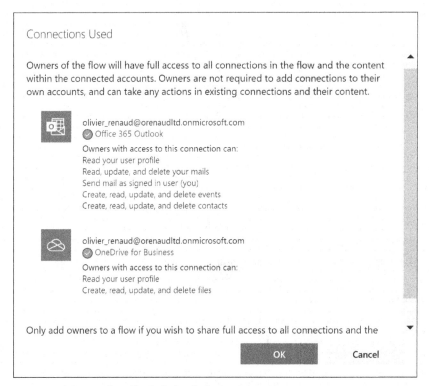

FIGURE 1-44 Connections Used window in Power Automate

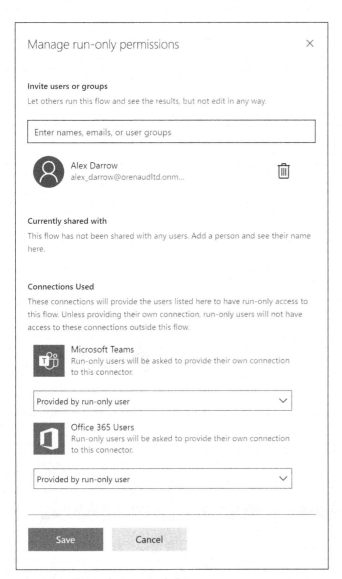

FIGURE 1-45 Run-only user permissions

Describe how to manage apps and users

While the administration of Power BI is relatively simple because the tool interacts with data sources on a read-only basis, Power Apps and Power Automate have the ability to modify data sources, and administrators must be more careful to regulate the privileges allotted to apps and users.

Managing apps

In the Power Apps portal, the Apps page, shown in Figure 1-46, allows you to select an app and edit it, run it, configure its settings, share it with other users, export it, add it to Microsoft Teams, or display its run history.

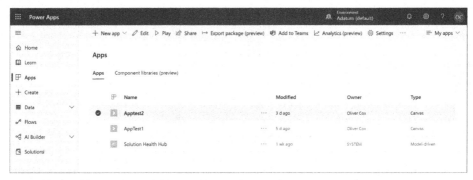

FIGURE 1-46 The Apps page in the Power Apps portal

Managing users

Because the Power Platform tools are all based on Microsoft Azure, they do not need their own identity subsystems; they use Azure Active Directory user accounts to control access to the tool portals and to the resources in each tool.

To create users and manage user account properties, administrators typically use the Microsoft 365 admin center, as shown in Figure 1-47.

After creating users, the administrator's next step in providing them with access to the Power Platform tools is to assign them the appropriate licenses, using the interface generated by the Manage product licenses button, as shown in Figure 1-48.

FIGURE 1-47 The Active users page in the Microsoft 365 admin center

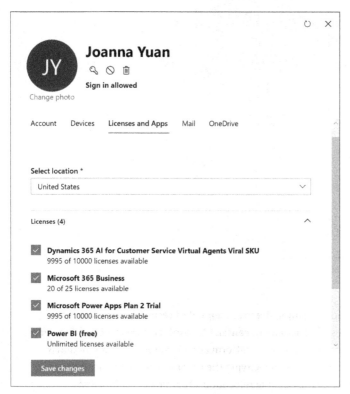

FIGURE 1-48 The Licenses and Apps tab for a selected user

The licenses available for assignment depend on the product subscriptions purchased by the tenant. The Power Platform tools have various levels of licensing, some of which are bundled with other products. For example, the Microsoft 365 and Dynamics 365 products include Power Apps and Power Automate (which may still be called Microsoft Flow). However, the capabilities of those versions are relatively limited compared with those of the standalone subscriptions, which must be purchased separately.

After assigning licenses, it might then be necessary for administrators to assign security roles to users. Security roles are associated with business units and are combinations of access levels and permissions that allow users to access data—such as data stored in the Microsoft Dataverse—to a specific degree. It is typically users who will be working with model apps for Dynamics 365 who require security roles.

The interface for the assignment of security roles is found in the Dynamics 365 user management center, as shown in Figure 1-49. This interface is accessible from the Power Platform admin center on the Settings/Security roles page for a selected environment.

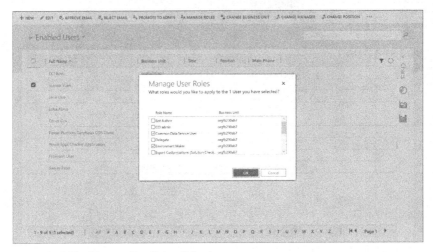

FIGURE 1-49 The Manage User Roles dialog box

Describe environments

When an administrator creates a tenancy in Azure Active Directory for any of the Power Platform tools or other Microsoft products, the software creates a default environment for that tenant. This initial environment is named for the tenant. An *environment* is a container for the apps and flows created in Power Apps and Power Automate, as well as the data they use. The Power Apps and Power Automate portals both display the current environment they are using in the upper right of the screen, as shown in Figure 1-50.

FIGURE 1-50 The environment indicator in the Power Apps portal

Because environments are associated with an Azure AD tenant, only the users in that tenancy can access the environment's resources. The environment is also bound to the tenant's geographical location.

Administrators can create only one Microsoft Dataverse database in a given environment. The data stored within that database is accessible only to apps and flows created in the same environment.

However, it is also possible for administrators to create additional environments. The Environments page in the Power Platform admin center, shown in Figure 1-51, lists all of the current tenant's environments.

FIGURE 1-51 The Environments page in the Power Platform admin center

Clicking the +New button opens the New environment dialog, as shown in Figure 1-52, in which the administrator specifies a name, type, and region for the environment. A second page contains options to specify the default language and currency values for the environment. In addition, there is a "Create a database for this environment?" control that causes the tool to create a Microsoft Dataverse database along with the environment.

FIGURE 1-52 Power Platform New environment dialog box

There are several reasons why administrators might want to create multiple environments in a particular tenancy. They can create separate environments for the teams, departments, or locations in an organization, or they might use them to separate app and flow development or testing projects from those released to production.

When creating an environment, an administrator must choose one of the following types:

- *Production*—Intended for permanent use and deployment; requires a Power Apps license and one gigabyte of storage space. The default environment created for each Azure AD tenant is a production environment.

- *Sandbox*—Intended for nonproduction use, such as for development and testing; includes functions to copy the contents of the environment to another environment and reset the environment to its original state by deleting all of its contents and re-creating it.

- *Trial*—Intended for short-term testing; limited to 30 days and one user.

- *Developer*—Intended for use only by the owner, who must possess a Community Plan license.

After an administrator has created multiple environments in a tenant, clicking the environment indicator in the Power Apps and Power Automate portals opens an Environments dialog that functions as a selector, as shown in Figure 1-53.

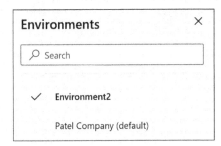

FIGURE 1-53 The Environments selector in the Power Apps portal

Describe where to perform specific administrative tasks, including Power Platform admin center and Microsoft 365 admin center

Microsoft Azure services typically have portals called admin centers that provide access to configuration settings, resources specific to the service, support topics, and links to other admin centers. For Microsoft 365 subscribers, the Microsoft 365 admin center is the primary configuration interface, enabling administrators to create and manage user accounts, purchase and manage product subscriptions, and access the other available admin centers, as shown in Figure 1-54.

The All admin centers list includes links to the admin centers for Power Automate, Power Apps, and Power BI. However, there is also an admin center for Power Platform, which does not appear on the list. The Power Platform admin center provides administrative access to the tenant's existing environments, as shown in Figure 1-55, as well as the ability to create new ones.

EXAM TIP

As of the second edition of this book, the Power Apps and Power Automate links on the All admin centers page lead to the Power Platform admin center. The Power Apps, Power Automate, and Dynamics 365 admin centers were all deprecated by Microsoft in June of 2020, but deprecated elements can remain usable for years before Microsoft removes them from the product. By the time you read this, the Power Apps and Power Automate admin centers might be gone completely, or just less accessible. If a function appears to have disappeared from one of the deprecated admin centers, the first place to go looking for it is the Power Platform admin center.

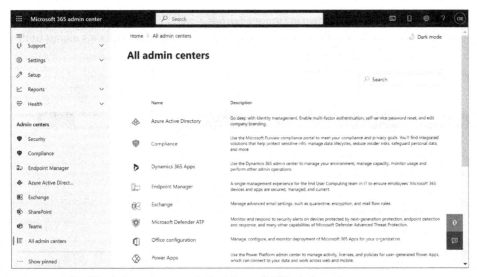

FIGURE 1-54 The All admin centers page in the Microsoft 365 admin center

The Analytics menu provides real-time statistics for the Power Platform tools, and the Admin centers menu provides links to the Power Automate, Power Apps, and Power BI admin centers, plus the Dynamics 365 admin center, if the organization subscribes to it. Microsoft is gradually migrating other functions from the Power Apps, Power Automate, and Dynamics 365 admin centers to the Power Platform admin center.

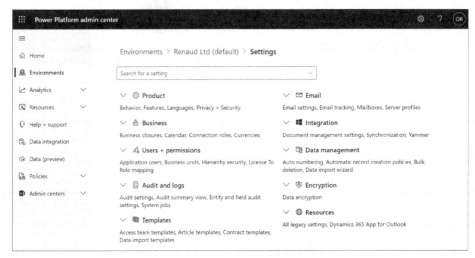

FIGURE 1-55 Environment Settings page in the Power Platform admin center

The Power BI Admin portal, shown in Figure 1-56, has a menu bar with 12 items, several of which display links to other admin centers. For example, the Users and Audit logs menus both link to the Microsoft 365 admin center, which is where you manage these elements. Other menus provide controls for features only available in the Power BI Premium product or that require the activation of other Microsoft Azure applications.

FIGURE 1-56 The Usage metrics page in the Power BI Admin portal

Describe data policies

The Power Platform tools are designed to access data from outside sources and, in some cases, write data back to those sources. Developers can create canvas apps and flows that access multiple data sources with different sensitivity levels. This process is inherently dangerous because the Power Platform content will eventually be deployed to consumers, who might or might not warrant direct access to sensitive data. Power Platform developers and administrators must exercise control over access to the data sources they use, and one method of doing so is to create data loss prevention policies.

Data loss prevention (DLP) policies are rules, created in the Power Platform admin center, that allow tenant admins and environment admins to classify connectors in three groups, as follows:

- *Non-business*—Intended for connectors that access non-sensitive data. Connectors in this group cannot share data with connectors in the Business group. A newly created DLP rule places all connectors in this category by default.

- *Business*—Intended for connectors that access sensitive data. Connectors in this group can share data with other connectors only in the Business group; they cannot share data with connectors in the Non-business group.

- *Blocked*—Intended for connectors that are not to be used in the environment at all.

To create DLP policies using the wizard in the Power Platform admin center, administrators assign the policy a name and use the interface shown in Figure 1-57 to move selected connectors from the Non-business group to the Business or Blocked group.

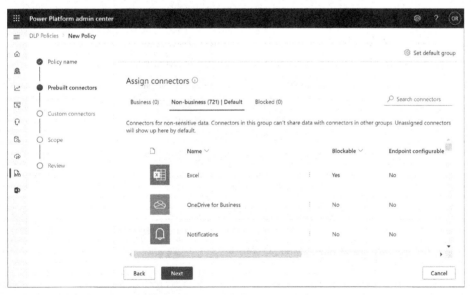

FIGURE 1-57 The Assign connectors page in the New Policy wizard

Then, using scope options, administrators can apply the new data policy to an entire tenancy or to specific environments within the tenancy.

Describe how Microsoft Power Platform supports privacy and accessibility guidelines

In any service or application that stores potentially sensitive data, and especially in cloud-based applications and services, there might be statutes and standards to which the organization must comply, whether because of contracted terms, company policies, or governmental requirements.

Microsoft is aware of these compliance issues and has created a central storehouse for information about them called the Service Trust Portal (STP). STP is a website that is available to everyone at servicetrust.microsoft.com, although some parts of the site are restricted to registered users of Microsoft 365 and other products. Among the many resources on the site are links to documents in the following categories:

- *Audit Reports*—Provides independent audit and assessment reports of Microsoft's cloud services, evaluating their compliance with standards such as those published by the International Organization for Standardization (ISO), Service Organization Controls (SOC), National Institute of Standards and Technology (NIST), Federal Risk and Authorization Management Program (FedRAMP), and General Data Protection Regulation (GDPR)

- *Documents & Resources*—Consists of a large library of documents, including white papers, FAQs, compliance guides, penetration test reports, Azure security and compliance blueprints, and other data protection resources

- *Compliance Manager*—A risk assessment tool that assesses and scores an organization's regulatory compliance, based on multiple published standards

- *Industries & Regions*—Provides documents containing compliance information for specific industries, such as education, financial services, government, health care, manufacturing, and retail, and specific countries, including Australia, Czech Republic, Germany, Poland, Romania, Spain, and the United Kingdom

- *Trust Center*—Links to the Trust Center site, which provides documentation on the means by which Microsoft supports security, privacy, compliance, and transparency in its cloud services

While the Service Trust Portal consists largely of documentary material, there are also some tools that administrators can use to assess their compliance with published standards and monitor the performance of their applications and services.

Compliance Manager

Compliance Manager is a risk assessment tool that allows an organization to track and record the activities they undertake to achieve compliance with specific certification standards. An assessment of an organization's compliance posture is based on the capabilities of the Microsoft cloud services and the ways that the organization makes use of them, as compared to an existing standard, regulation, or law.

The home page for the Compliance Manager tool contains a dashboard that displays tiles representing the assessments of the selected components against different standards, as shown in Figure 1-58. Each tile specifies a cloud service and the specific standard to which it is being compared. The results of the comparison are stated as a numerical score.

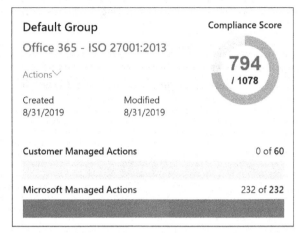

Default Group	Compliance Score
Office 365 - ISO 27001:2013	
Actions⌄	**794** / **1078**
Created 8/31/2019	Modified 8/31/2019
Customer Managed Actions	0 of **60**
Microsoft Managed Actions	232 of **232**

FIGURE 1-58 A Compliance Manager tile

Selecting a tile displays a list of the cloud services being tested for the assessment, as shown in Figure 1-59, along with the results for each individual control. The controls are broken down into those for which Microsoft is responsible and those for which the customer is responsible. Each control entry contains a reference to a section or article in the standard that corresponds to the control; information about who tested the control and when; and the results of the test, expressed as an individual Compliance Score value.

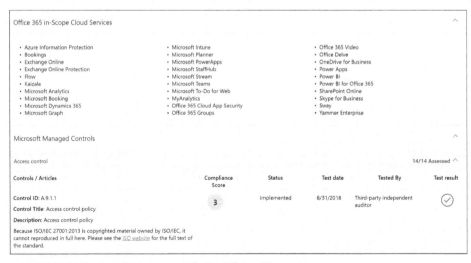

FIGURE 1-59 A cloud service assessment in Compliance Manager

Auditing

Power Platform also supports auditing, which is another way of monitoring compliance with data access regulations. Auditing captures instances of specific activities and saves them to a log file, which administrators can review to monitor data access by specific users, modifications of security roles, changes made to entities and fields, changes made to sharing privileges, and the time and place of updates.

To allow auditing and to access auditing logs, an administrator expands the Audit and logs heading on an environment's Settings page in the Power Platform admin center. Selecting Audit settings opens the Auditing tab on the System Settings page of the Dynamics 365 admin center, as shown in Figure 1-60.

FIGURE 1-60 The Auditing tab of the System Settings page in the Dynamics 365 admin center

Other controls on the environment's Settings page allow administrators to manage the logs and view individual entries, as shown in Figure 1-61.

FIGURE 1-61 Audit log detail

Describe Microsoft Power Platform governance capabilities

The no-code/low-code philosophy behind the Power Platform tools can certainly increase the efficiency of the development process, increase productivity, and lower development costs, but it also raises governance issues. When the development and administration of Power Platform content falls outside of the IT infrastructure, who is ultimately responsible for the development process and the security of the resulting content? How can IT ensure that licensing and security procedures are observed with regard to any potentially sensitive data used in the creation of Power Platform content? In short, who owns the apps, flows, dashboards, and reports, IT or the "citizen developers?"

A lack of governance in a Power Platform implementation can result in any or all of the following issues:

- Orphaned apps—When citizen developers create apps or flows, they presumably take charge of maintaining and updating them afterward. What happens when the owner of an app or flow leaves the company? IT-governed software usually has a protocol in place for handing off ownership to others, but the need for such a protocol might not even occur to non-IT developers, resulting in apps and flows that are left without owners and access to administrative functions.

- Compromised data—Citizen developers might, in many cases, be more concerned with getting an app or flow to function than with maintaining a secure system of ownerships and permissions. The result could be data left unprotected and open to compromise. The complicated interaction of apps, flows, connectors, and the Microsoft Dataverse can make the issues of credentials and permissions problematic.

- Unused features—The Power Platform tools typically have internal capabilities that can enable citizen developers to address the most prevalent governance problems, but a non-IT developer might not be aware of those capabilities. When people from other departments are compelled to undertake a software development effort, it is not unusual for them to be more concerned with getting the task accomplished than with conforming to the best practices for software development.

- Slow flows—Automated flows are intended to speed up business processes and increase productivity, but there are several conditions that can cause flows to run slowly, sometimes even more slowly than the manual processes they replace. Citizen developers might not be aware of data consumption limits or Power Platform licensing issues that restrict the execution of particular actions. These are standard concerns that IT-based developers address as a matter of course, but non-IT developers might not be conscious of them until a problem occurs.

- Flow errors—Flows can encounter run-time errors that stop them from executing until the error condition is addressed. A flow might test correctly during its development, but conditions can change, and errors could crop up later. How the flow handles potential error conditions is another element of the development process that IT personnel probably handle regularly, but which might escape the citizen developer. Depending on its function, a flow that stops executing due to an error can have a negative effect on productivity that makes the solution worse than the manual procedure that was the original problem Power Automate was supposed to solve.

Microsoft's solution for establishing governance policies for Power Platform is called the Center of Excellence (CoE) Starter Kit. Available as a free download, the CoE kit consists of various dashboards, apps, and flows that take inventory of the enterprise and provide administrators with a detailed view of the Power Platform resources currently in use, as shown in Figure 1-62.

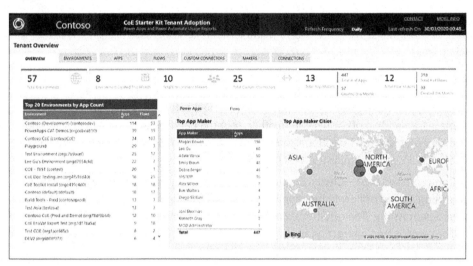

FIGURE 1-62 CoE Starter Kit dashboard

The various screens display lists of all the relevant Power Platform components, including environments, makers, apps, flows, and connectors. Other components provide solutions for the problems listed earlier, such as controls that enable administrators to locate orphaned apps and assign new owners to them. It is also possible to establish compliance policies for the citizen developers in the organization so that they can be aware of the potential problems that can arise.

The CoE Starter Kit is not a complete solution. As the name implies, it is just a beginning framework for an organization to use when creating governance policies for Power Platform. Every organization has its own governance requirements, so the kit provides the tools to manage Power Platform across the enterprise, but it is still up to IT and the citizen developers to make use of them.

Describe analytics and how they can be used

The Power Platform admin center includes an Analytics menu that enables administrators to monitor usage settings and other metrics for Microsoft Dataverse, Power Apps, and Power Automate, as shown in Figure 1-63. Each of the Analytics pages has multiple tabs that display statistical information in Power BI dashboard format, with various types of cards and graphs that update in real time.

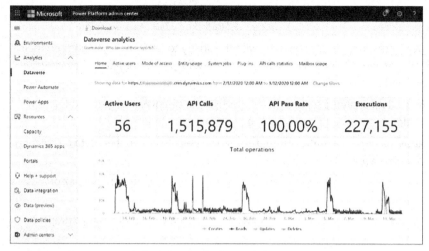

FIGURE 1-63 Dataverse analytics in Power Platform admin center

In addition to the pages for Dataverse, Power Automate, and Power Apps analytics, administrators can enable tenant-level analytics from the Power Platform settings dialog box, as shown in Figure 1-64. Once enabled, a drop-down menu appears in the upper right corner of the Power Apps analytics page, enabling the user to choose between Environment level analytics and Tenant level analytics. Switching to Tenant level analytics modifies the display to show metrics for all of the environments in the tenancy combined.

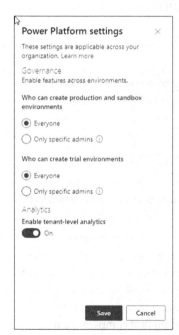

FIGURE 1-64 Power Platform settings in Power Platform admin center

Chapter summary

- The Power Platform tools provide users with the ability to perform key actions on their data: analyze it with Power BI, create apps with Power Apps, automate tasks with Power Automate, and create chatbots with Power Virtual Agents.

- Power BI is a data analytics service that allows users to discover and gather data from local and cloud sources and then visualize and share that data.

- Power Apps is a development platform that allows users to act on their data by creating web and mobile applications without writing code.

- Power Automate is an automation service that allows users to trigger complex processes and workflows.

- Power Virtual Agents is a service that allows users to create chatbots using a graphical interface with no coding.

- Power Platform provides connectivity both within and among the various applications and services in Dynamics 365, Microsoft 365, Microsoft Azure, and other third-party products.

- The Power Platform tools—Power BI, Power Apps, Power Automate, and Power Virtual Agents, along with their underlying components (Microsoft Dataverse, data connectors, and AI Builder)—run as individual services, meaning that they are cloud-based software products that are hosted by Microsoft Azure on a software as a service (SaaS) basis.

- All of the Power Platform tools rely on Azure Active Directory for user accounts and licensing.

- The Power Platform admin center provides administrative access to the tenant's existing environments, as well as the ability to create new ones.

- Compliance Manager is a risk assessment tool that allows an organization to track and record the activities they undertake to achieve compliance with specific certification standards.

Thought experiment

In this thought experiment, demonstrate your skills and knowledge of the topics covered in this chapter. You can find the answer to this thought experiment in the next section.

Ralph is the sole IT administrator for Wingtip Toys, which has six offices in different cities. The offices have always operated independently, with each one maintaining its own financial information using Excel workbooks. The company executives are concerned about the security of their financial data. This is one of the reasons each of the six offices maintains its own Excel workbooks. Because of this arrangement, creating a picture of the company's overall financial health has always been a problem. Each year, an outside accounting firm compiles the data from the six offices into a comprehensive report, a process that is expensive and time-consuming and that generates a financial picture that is largely out of date.

Ralph has been asked to devise a solution that will provide the company executives with an overall financial picture of the entire company that is updated on a continual basis. Having seen materials on the Power BI service, Ralph thinks that it might help him to accomplish his task.

Based on Ralph's requirements and your knowledge of the Power BI service, which of the following are true statements?

1. Power BI is capable of accessing data from six different Excel workbooks at different locations and combining the data into a single financial report display that is accessible from any internet device.

2. Power BI can access the Excel data from the six sites without any possible danger of the original files being modified or damaged.

3. Ralph can use Power BI Desktop to create new reports on his Android smartphone and publish them to the Power BI service.

4. Ralph must manually update the Power BI reports he creates to make sure that the data displayed is current.

Thought experiment answers

This section contains the solution to the thought experiment. Each answer explains why the answer choice is correct.

1. True. Power BI provides access to more than 200 data sources that allow designers to obtain data from Excel workbooks on local network computers, as well as from network services such as SQL databases and from cloud-based services such as SharePoint and Google Analytics.

2. True. Power BI consists of services, applications, and connectors that can access data from multiple sources and display it in various ways, but Power BI does not manipulate or modify the original data in any way. Whether a user is a designer using Power BI Desktop to model data or a consumer using the Power BI reading view to display the published data, nothing that either type of user does can possibly modify or delete the underlying data itself.

3. False. Power BI Desktop is a free Windows application that designers can use to create Power BI content and publish it on the Power BI Service for consumers to use. It cannot run on an Android smartphone.

4. False. After a designer connects to a data source, creates Power BI content, and publishes it to the service, the connection to the source remains in place and the published data is updated automatically as the source data changes. This allows users to track information on a continual basis.

CHAPTER 2

Identify the core components of Microsoft Power Platform

Microsoft Power Platform consists of primary applications such as Power BI, Power Apps, Power Automate, and Power Virtual Agents. However, there are also underlying technologies that all the applications can use, including the Microsoft Dataverse database, a collection of data connectors, and the AI Builder automation and intelligence engine, as shown in Figure 2-1.

Microsoft Power Platform

The low code platform that spans Microsoft 365, Azure, Dynamics 365, and standalone apps.

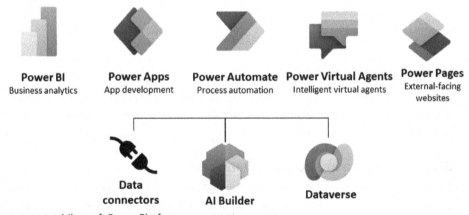

Power BI
Business analytics

Power Apps
App development

Power Automate
Process automation

Power Virtual Agents
Intelligent virtual agents

Power Pages
External-facing websites

Data connectors

AI Builder

Dataverse

FIGURE 2-1 Microsoft Power Platform components

Skills covered in this chapter:

- Skill 2.1: Describe Microsoft Dataverse
- Skill 2.2: Describe connectors

Skill 2.1: Describe Microsoft Dataverse

Microsoft Dataverse is a cloud-based data storage solution that all the Power Platform applications can use to maintain their data in a secure, manageable environment. The Microsoft Dataverse was originally designed for use with Dynamics 365 applications, such as Sales and Customer Service. Therefore, Power Platform developers can use their existing Dynamics 365 business data, logic, and F0rules when creating new content in Power BI, Power Apps, and Power Automate.

This skill covers how to:

- Introduce Microsoft Dataverse
- Describe the difference between databases and Dataverse
- Describe the differences between Dataverse and Dataverse for Teams
- Describe tables, columns, and relationships
- Describe how to use common standard tables to describe people, places, and things
- Describe business logic uses, including business rules, real-time workflows, and actions
- Describe dataflows and their uses
- Describe solutions and their purpose

Introduce Microsoft Dataverse

Power Apps and the other Power Platform tools require data for developers to work with, and they are all able to connect directly to many different data sources, including local files, network resources, and cloud-based services.

Storing app data in Microsoft Dataverse

Depending on the nature of the app they are building, it is common for developers to connect to multiple data sources to gather the information they need. This can mean accessing multiple sites, authenticating with multiple accounts, and updating multiple data points at frequent intervals. Microsoft Dataverse can simplify this data gathering model by allowing developers to store the data from the different sources in a single protected place, in an integrated form. The data stored in Microsoft Dataverse is then available to any of the Power Platform tools, along with any Dynamics 365 data that is also stored there.

For example, when an organization relies heavily on data stored in many Excel workbooks, importing them one time into Microsoft Dataverse can be more convenient than connecting to each one repeatedly every time an app is revised or updated. When importing data into

Microsoft Dataverse, developers can model and transform the data using Power Query, just as they can when importing data using Power BI.

NEED MORE REVIEW? **DATA MODELING AND TRANSFORMATION**

For more information on data modeling and transformation, see "Skill 3.2: Connect to and consume data" in Chapter 3, "Describe the business value of Power BI."

As with direct connections between apps and data sources, Microsoft Dataverse can synchronize with the data sources at regular intervals to keep the stored data updated. The apps that use the Microsoft Dataverse data can then be updated with the latest information as well.

Using Microsoft Dataverse with canvas and model apps

As mentioned in Chapter 1, "Describe the business value of Microsoft Power Platform," Power Apps supports two basic app types for internal users: canvas and model apps. (A third type, portal apps, is intended to create websites for external users.)

Canvas apps are relatively simple and give the developer a great deal of control over the user experience the app provides. Power Apps offers canvas apps with standard functions such as read, write, search, and delete based on the structure of the data used by the app. Developers can use Power Platform connectors to access data sources directly, or they can use Microsoft Dataverse. It is possible to create more complex canvas apps, but the configuration process can become time-consuming for the developer.

Model apps are typically more complex than canvas apps, and they always use Microsoft Dataverse as a data source. Model apps also have less flexibility as far as the user experience is concerned; they use the Dynamics 365 framework. After the developer has created the data model, Power Apps generates a user interface that is appropriate for it. In fact, some of the Dynamics 365 Customer Engagement modules are essentially model-driven Power Apps. This makes it easier for developers to create more complex apps than it would be to manually create them from a blank canvas.

Describe the difference between databases and Dataverse

Microsoft Dataverse is frequently referred to as a database, in documentation and even in this book, but it is actually much more than that. Dataverse is often compared with SQL Server, as though the two are equivalents, but while the actual databases the two products create are similar in structure, Dataverse is fully integrated into Microsoft's cloud infrastructure. Hosted by Microsoft Azure, Dataverse utilizes many of Azure's services, not just to store data but also to provide data modeling, security, and integration with Microsoft 365 services. To implement in SQL Server what Microsoft Dataverse includes as standard features would require a substantial integration and development effort.

Figure 2-2 illustrates the many capabilities that Microsoft Dataverse provides to Power Platform developers and consumers.

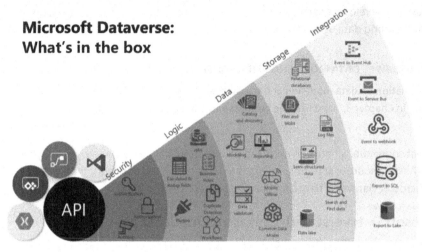

Microsoft Dataverse: What's in the box

FIGURE 2-2 Microsoft Dataverse is fully integrated into the Azure cloud infrastructure

The diagram divides the Dataverse capabilities into five categories, as follows:

- Security—Azure Active Directory (AD) provides identity services, including authentication, authorization, and accounting, for Microsoft Dataverse and all of the Power Platform tools.

- Logic—Dataverse can apply business logic at the data level so that the rules are enforced no matter how users and apps are accessing the data.

- Data—Dataverse and Power Platform provide data modeling, transformation, and reporting tools, enabling users to alter the presentation of the data as needed.

- Storage—All Dataverse data is stored in the Azure cloud, with all of the security, protection, and fault tolerance that entails.

- Integration—Dataverse is integrated with the Microsoft 365 services hosted by Azure, including Office, SharePoint, Exchange, and OneDrive.

While SQL Server and other database management products might provide some of these services to a degree, none of them can provide the same capabilities as Microsoft Dataverse "out of the box."

Describe the differences between Dataverse and Dataverse for Teams

When a user creates an app or flow within Microsoft Teams for the first time or installs an app from the app catalog, Teams creates a Dataverse for Teams environment to support it. Dataverse for Teams is a separate implementation of Microsoft Dataverse that performs the same basic functions for that particular team as the Dataverse does for a Power Platform environment. Dataverse for Teams stores the team's data, apps, flows, and bots and makes them available to other team members. Dataverse for Teams is provided with most of the Microsoft 365 licenses that include Microsoft Teams

The environment that Microsoft Teams creates appears on the Environments page in the Power Platform admin center, as shown in Figure 2-3, with Microsoft Teams listed as its type. However, the apps and flows that users create in Teams do not appear in the Power Apps portal or the Power Apps mobile app.

FIGURE 2-3 A Dataverse for Teams environment in the Power Platform admin center

The apps and flows stored in a Dataverse for Teams environment are accessible to team members using links from within Teams or, when outside of Teams, through a web browser, as long as the user has a standalone Power Apps license. Team members can also invite guests and provide them with the ability to discover and run the apps, flows, and bots in the Database for Teams environment. However, the guests cannot create or modify apps and flows.

The Dataverse for Teams environment has no application programming interface (API) access and is available only to apps, flows, and bots within that environment. Storage is limited to 2 gigabytes per team, with up to one million table rows. The license supports up to five teams, with one additional team for every 20 licenses purchased.

If API access is needed, or if the environment's storage limit is reached, or if users need to access the apps, flows, and bots using the standalone Power Platform tools, it is possible for a tenant admin to upgrade the Dataverse for Teams environment to a standard Microsoft Dataverse environment using the Power Platform admin center portal.

Describe tables, columns, and relationships

Microsoft Dataverse is a cloud-based data storage solution, which means it is available to any users with internet access and appropriate credentials. As with most of Microsoft's cloud-based products, Microsoft Dataverse uses Azure Active Directory (AAD) for user authentication and authorization. Organizations that are Microsoft 365 subscribers can use their same user accounts to access Microsoft Dataverse data; Dynamics 365 subscribers are already accessing their Microsoft Dataverse data with their AAD user accounts.

Power Platform developers can create multiple Dataverse database instances to accommodate the needs of various apps and users. Each database instance can support up to 4 terabytes of storage; additional storage is also available for purchase.

EXAM TIP

Since the publication of this book in its first edition, Microsoft has made substantial changes to the terminology used in Power Platform. What used to be called the Common Data Service is now Microsoft Dataverse, and the elements of the databases it creates have also been renamed, as follows:

What used to be called:	Is now called:
Common Data Service	Microsoft Dataverse
Entities	Tables
Fields	Columns
Records	Rows

While much of Microsoft's own documentation has already been updated with the new terminology, there are still a great many sources that have not. Candidates for the PL-900 exam should be conscious of these modifications when selecting preparation materials.

Using tables

When a developer creates a database instance in Microsoft Dataverse, it consists of a standard set of tables, with each table having a standard set of columns. A default Microsoft Dataverse instance has a base set of standard tables, some of which are shown in Figure 2-4, any of which the developer can select and populate with data from an outside source.

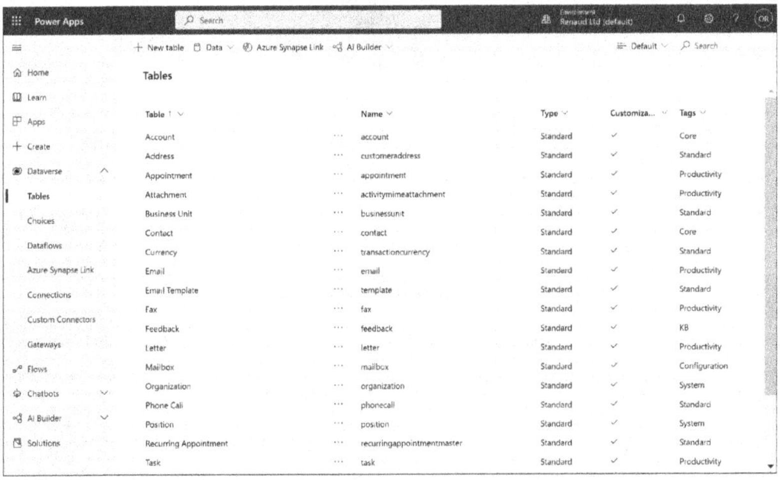

FIGURE 2-4 Standard tables in a Microsoft Dataverse instance

In addition to the standard tables created with every Microsoft Dataverse instance, developers can create custom tables to suit the requirements of specific business applications, assuming that none of the standard ones are suitable. It is possible to rename a standard table if that makes it more suitable to the application that will use it.

Creating a custom table is simply a matter of clicking the +New table button on the Tables screen in the Power Apps portal to open the dialog box shown in Figure 2-5 and supplying a name for the table. After expanding the More settings header, the developer can specify the table type and the ownership option. After the developer has created the new table in the Power Apps portal, they can create custom columns within it.

Aside from the Standard table type, the developer can also choose the Activity table type, which is a table that can manage tasks for which it is possible to create a calendar entry, such as appointments, phone calls, faxes, and emails.

The other option for the Standard table type is its ownership, which has the following options:

- *User or team*—Actions that developers can perform on this table's records are controlled at the user level. User or team ownership is the only possible option for Activity tables.

- *Organization*—Access to the data stored in the table is controlled at the organization level.

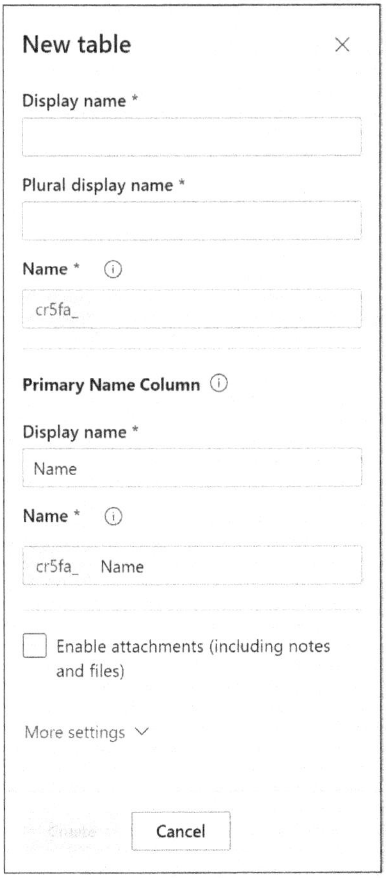

New table   ✕

Display name *

_____

Plural display name *

_____

Name *   ⓘ

cr5fa_

Primary Name Column ⓘ

Display name *

Name

Name *   ⓘ

cr5fa_   Name

☐ Enable attachments (including notes and files)

More settings ∨

[Create] [Cancel]

FIGURE 2-5 New table dialog box in the Power Apps portal

Using columns

Columns are the attributes within a table that contain specific types of data. Just as an entity in the Common Data Service is the equivalent of a table in Microsoft Dataverse, a field in an entity is the equivalent of a column in a table, which contains a particular data point for each record, represented by a row in the table. For example, every table has an Address column by default, which is configured with a data type called Multiline Text, indicating that every value for that column can consist of one or more lines of plain text. Other columns might have data types such as Whole Number, Date and Time, or Phone.

Just as a standard set of tables exists in every database instance, a standard set of columns exists in every table, as shown in Figure 2-6. Depending on the table, there can be just a few standard columns or over a hundred.

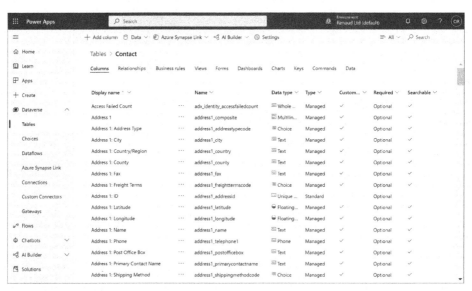

FIGURE 2-6 Standard columns in a Microsoft Dataverse table

Developers can often use the standard columns for most purposes, but when they cannot, it is possible to create customized columns. Clicking the +Add column button on a table page in the Power Apps portal opens the Column properties dialog box, as shown in Figure 2-7.

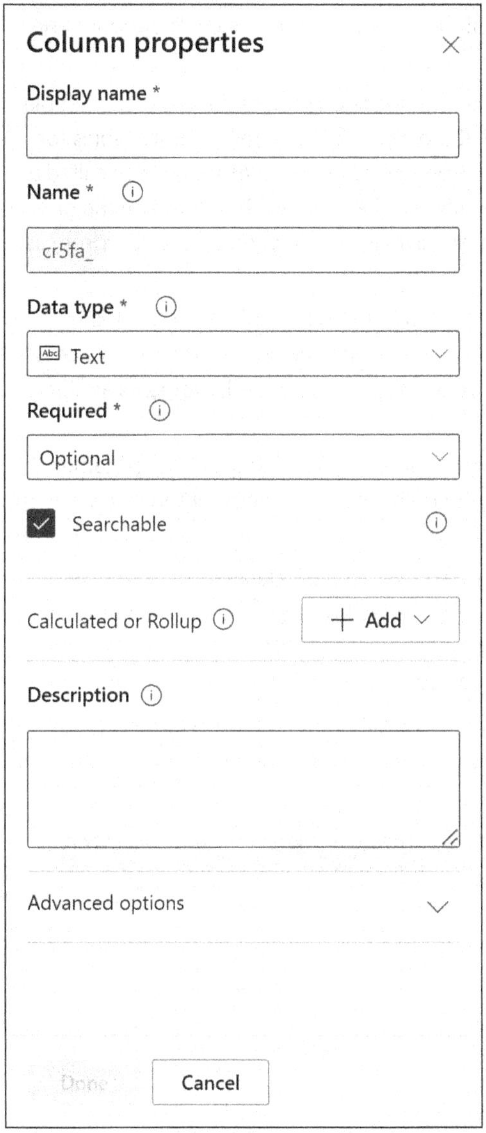

Column properties ✕

Display name *

Name * ⓘ

cr5fa_

Data type * ⓘ

[Abc] Text ⌄

Required * ⓘ

Optional ⌄

☑ Searchable ⓘ

Calculated or Rollup ⓘ   + Add ⌄

Description ⓘ

Advanced options ⌄

Done   Cancel

FIGURE 2-7 Column properties dialog box in the Power Apps portal

Understanding relationships

Depending on the nature of the app a developer is creating and the data that it will use, it might be a good idea to create multiple tables to hold different types of data, rather than store many different data types in a single table.

For example, in the case of an order entry app, the developer might need to maintain a list of incoming invoices and a list of the products ordered on each invoice. The database for this app would therefore need—at minimum—records for the invoices and records for the products ordered. There would presumably also need to be records for customer information and records for an inventory of products. Storing all of this information in a single table would be complicated at best.

To better organize the data for the app, it would therefore be preferable to create multiple tables and establish relationships between them. If the developer creates separate tables for the invoices and the products ordered, there could be said to be a *one-to-many* (also called a parent/child or 1:N) relationship between the two tables. The invoice table would be the one (or the parent), and the products table could contain as many product records (or children) as are needed for each invoice.

In the same way, the invoice table can have a *many-to-one* (N:1) relationship to a table containing customer information. Each customer can have many invoices, but each invoice is associated with only one customer. This type of relationship between tables appears as a field type called a *lookup field*.

Microsoft Dataverse also supports *many-to-many* (or N:N) relationships between tables, in which many records in one table are associated with many records in another table, in what are known as *peer relationships*.

As mentioned earlier, the standard tables provided by Microsoft Dataverse are sufficient for the needs of most developers and their apps, and the relationships between the tables are already in place. Selecting any table in the Power Apps portal and selecting the Relationships tab displays the existing relationships and their types, as shown in Figure 2-8.

From this screen, it is also possible for developers to create new relationships by clicking the +Add relationship button and choosing Many-to-one, One-to-many, or Many-to-many, to open a dialog box like the one shown in Figure 2-9.

FIGURE 2-8 The Relationships tab for the Contact table in the Power Apps portal

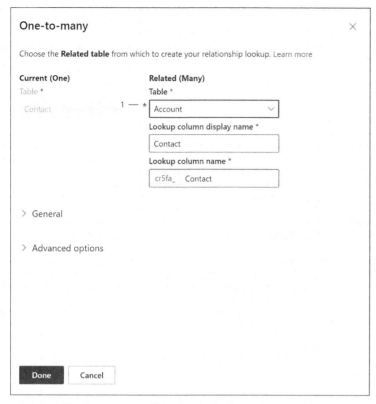

FIGURE 2-9 The One-to-many dialog box in the Power Apps portal

Describe how to use common standard tables to describe people, places, and things

As mentioned earlier in this chapter, creating a Microsoft Dataverse instance in an environment automatically populates the database with a collection of standard tables that are designed to support the most commonly used types of business data, including the following:

- Account
- Address
- Appointment
- Attachment
- Business Unit
- Contact
- Currency
- Email
- Feedback

- Letter
- Mailbox
- Organization
- Phone call
- Position
- Task
- Team
- User

These tables represent people, places, and things, elements that many businesses use on a daily basis when communicating both internally and outside the organization. Each table includes columns appropriate to its subject, as shown in Figure 2-10. The standard tables are all customizable, making it possible for developers to add new columns or modify existing ones as needed.

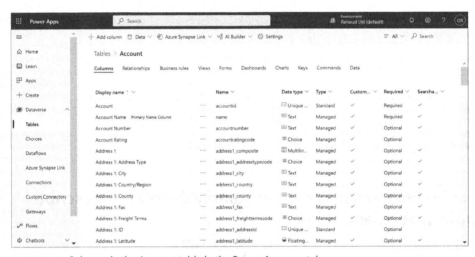

FIGURE 2-10 Columns in the Account table in the Power Apps portal

NEED MORE REVIEW? **STANDARD TABLES**

For more information on standard tables, see "Describe tables, columns, and relationships," earlier in this chapter.

Describe business logic uses, including business rules, real-time workflows, and actions

Power Apps provides several mechanisms that developers can use to implement business logic in their apps, including business rules, workflows, and actions. These mechanisms are described in the following sections.

Business rules

Business rules enable developers to implement business logic on data stored in the Microsoft Dataverse. Because the rules apply to the data, and not to a specific app, they take effect however the data is used. For example, if the value of the Country field in a table is entered as Canada, a business rule can enable a six-digit alphanumeric Postal Code field and hide the five-digit numeric Zip Code field used for US addresses.

Business rules consist of conditions and actions. *Conditions* are circumstances that must be met for the rule to apply, and *actions* are the procedures taken when the circumstances of the condition are met. When a developer opens a table in the Power Apps portal and selects New > Business Rule, a New business rule canvas appears, as shown in Figure 2-11.

As with a business process flow, developers can drag elements from the Components pane to the canvas. Selecting an element on the canvas causes the Properties interface for that element to appear in the right pane. The combination of conditions and actions creates an IF/THEN logic statement that appears in the Business Rule (Text View) box on the canvas.

For a condition, the developer configures one or more rules specifying when the actions should occur. In the figure, the condition calls for the Country field to have the value Canada. When that condition is met, the specified actions occur. The developer can then create actions that cause the US Zip Code field to be hidden and the Canadian-format Postal Code field to be shown.

Conditions can be more complex, with multiple rules that use Boolean AND/OR operators to specify whether both conditions, or either one of the conditions, must be met for the actions to apply. The rule can also include multiple actions that execute when the condition is met.

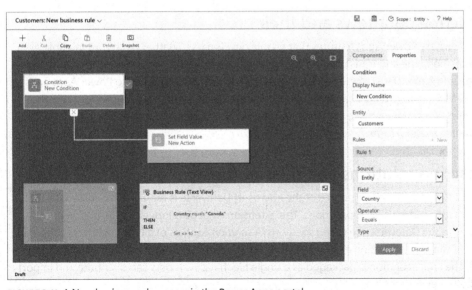

FIGURE 2-11 A New business rule canvas in the Power Apps portal

The most common functions of business rules are to simplify the process of supplying data for users and verify the accuracy of the data that users supply. To that end, developers can create rules that set values for fields, clear the values from fields, and validate the data entered into fields. In model-driven apps (only), business rules can also show, hide, enable, and disable fields. For example, when users are required to supply their annual income in a field, a rule can enable additional fields for verification if the income exceeds a specified amount.

Real-time workflows

Real-time workflows are a means of automating repetitive processes on tables that do not require user interaction. Workflows, like business processes, are organized into stages, each of which has a series of steps. The steps can cause the workflow to create, update, and assign table rows, as well as launch other workflows. Another type of workflow, the *background workflow*, is run by Power Automate.

Actions

Actions, also known as custom actions or custom process actions, are similar to real-time workflows in that they are divided into stages and steps and consist of conditions and actions. Custom actions expand the native capabilities of Power Platform by creating custom messages. Power Apps has built-in messages that use verbs such as Create, Update, and Delete. With custom actions, users can create additional messages that consist of multiple steps, resulting in new verbs, such as Approve, Escalate, or Convert.

Describe dataflows and their uses

Dataflows are Power Apps features that enable developers to gather data from multiple sources, combine and transform the data, and store it in a table, either in the Microsoft Dataverse or in Azure Data Lake Storage. Once stored, the data is accessible to Power Apps apps and refreshed according to a schedule specified by the developer. Other developers in the organization can then make use of the dataflow with assurance that it is up to date and organized into a useful form.

Describe solutions and their purpose

One of the basic design principles of the Microsoft Dataverse is the ability to customize the database to suit specific applications. The extensions that developers create, package, and deploy to the Dataverse are called solutions. A *solution* consists of all the customizations made to the Dataverse, including any modifications that developers might make to an existing solution. The entire solution is packaged as a single file that developers can distribute and import into other environments.

Solutions can contain a variety of components generated by the Power Platform tools, including Power Apps canvas apps and model-driven apps, Power Automate flows, custom connectors, and Dataverse tables. However, solutions do not contain any business data.

Developers can create two types of solutions, as follows:

- *Unmanaged*—Intended for development environments in which modifications are being made to the solution. Developers can export an unmanaged solution as either a managed or unmanaged solution. After a developer imports an unmanaged solution, deleting the solution causes the solution file to be deleted, but the customizations applied to the environment remain in place.

- *Managed*—Intended for nondevelopment situations, such as test and production environments. Developers cannot export a managed solution or edit the components in a managed solution directly; they must first add the components to an unmanaged solution, which is editable. Deleting a managed solution causes all of the customizations included in the solution to be removed from the environment.

The typical progression is for developers to create and refine an unmanaged solution in a development environment and then export it as a managed solution for deployment in a test environment and later a production environment, as shown in Figure 2-12.

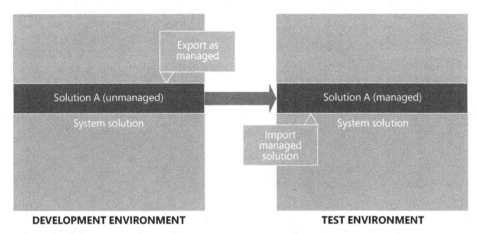

DEVELOPMENT ENVIRONMENT **TEST ENVIRONMENT**

FIGURE 2-12 Development progression using unmanaged and managed solutions

To create a solution, a developer clicks the New solution button on the Solutions page in the Power Apps portal to open the dialog box shown in Figure 2-13. After the solution is created, the developer can then create components or add existing ones. Developers can employ solutions in a variety of use cases, including application lifecycle management and business process flows.

FIGURE 2-13 The New solution dialog box in the Power Apps portal

Skill 2.2: Describe connectors

Connectors are the Power Platform components that allow Power Apps and Power Automate to interact with outside applications, services, and data files and utilize their data. Hundreds of public connectors are available to Power Platform users, and for those applications and services that are not supported, it is possible for developers to create custom connectors.

A *connector* is a proxy wrapper that Power Platform tools use to access an application programming interface (API) provided by an application or service. Many applications and cloud services have the necessary APIs, and the Power Platform connectors function as *proxies*, or intermediaries between the outside APIs and the internal Power Platform tools. The connector, in its role as a proxy, authenticates to the outside application or service and then provides Power Apps and Power Automate with access to its data.

> **This section covers how to:**
> - Describe triggers, including trigger types and where triggers are used
> - Describe actions
> - Describe licensing options for connectors, including standard or premium tier
> - Identify use cases for custom connectors

Describe triggers, including trigger types and where triggers are used

Triggers are components in Power Automate that cause a flow to begin running. Some triggers can be schedule based, so that the flow launches at a specific date and time; others can be event based, so that the flow launches when a user performs a specific task, or even manual, in which a user launches a flow by clicking or tapping a button. However, there are also triggers associated with data connectors, so that changes involving a data source cause a flow to launch.

For example, the connector for SharePoint includes triggers that can launch a flow when an item is created, when an item is created or modified, or when a file is created in a folder, as shown in Figure 2-14.

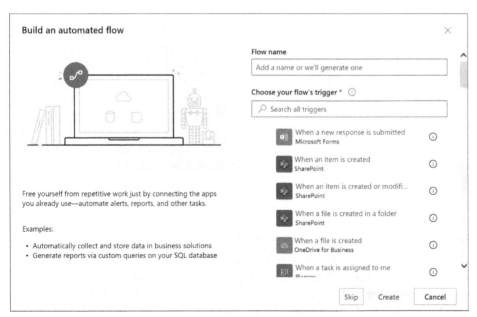

FIGURE 2-14 The Build an automated flow dialog box from the Power Automate portal

When a developer creates an automated flow—that is, a flow that is launched by an outside event—two types of triggers are available:

- *Polling triggers*—Connect to the outside data source at scheduled intervals to check for new data, launching the flow using that new data as input when it becomes available

- *Push triggers*—Listen at a server endpoint for notifications that a specific event has occurred on an outside application or service, launching the flow when the notification arrives

When developers create instant flows or scheduled flows, they still use triggers, but these triggers function autonomously. An instant flow uses a trigger that is tied to a button or other control in an app that requires user interaction to launch the flow. Scheduled flows use a trigger that the developer configures to activate at a specific date and time, using the interface shown in Figure 2-15.

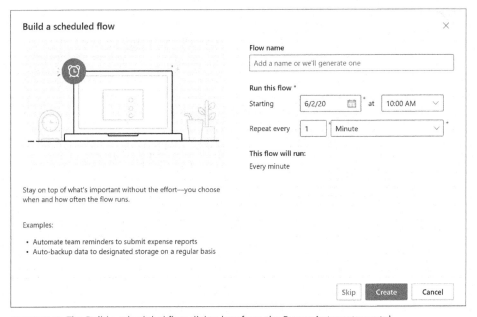

FIGURE 2-15 The Build a scheduled flow dialog box from the Power Automate portal

Describe actions

Actions are specific modifications made to the data provided by an outside application or service. In Power Automate, actions are usually the result of a trigger, but developers can use them in Power Apps as well. For example, when a developer creates a manual trigger in a Power Automate flow, the next step is to select an action that will be the result of the trigger, as shown in Figure 2-16. Apps and flows can include multiple actions using different connectors to perform a sequence of tasks.

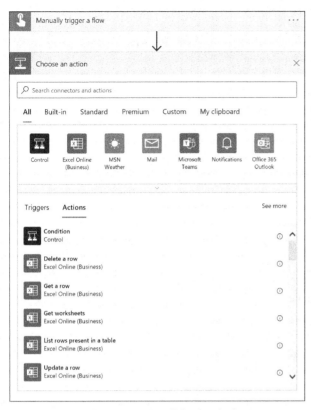

FIGURE 2-16 The Choose an action dialog box in the Power Automate portal

Actions can cause an application or service to perform a task, such as send an email, or modify the source data in some way. For example, Figure 2-17 contains the interface for an action that deletes a row from a specific Excel spreadsheet.

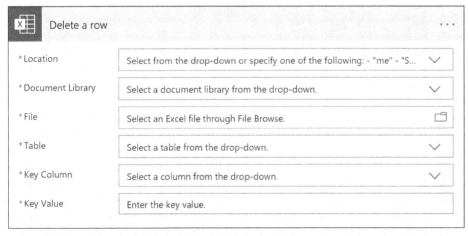

FIGURE 2-17 The Delete a row action for Excel in the Power Automate portal

The developer uses the interface to specify the location of the Excel file, identify the worksheet in the file on which the action will be performed, and specify the row to be deleted. Other actions for the Excel connector make it possible to get data from a worksheet or update a worksheet with new data supplied by the app or flow. The actions for the many other connectors depend on the capabilities of the application or service.

Describe licensing options for connectors, including standard or premium tier

As mentioned earlier, Power Platform provides connectors for over 200 applications and services, and Microsoft is regularly adding new ones. There are two classes of connectors, standard and premium, access to which is based on the Power Apps or Power Automate license in use.

Standard connectors are available to all licensees of Power Apps and Power Automate, regardless of the plan or product through which the user obtained the license. The standard connectors include those for many of the Microsoft 365 and Office 365 applications and services, as well as for popular social media services, a sampling of which is shown in Figure 2-18.

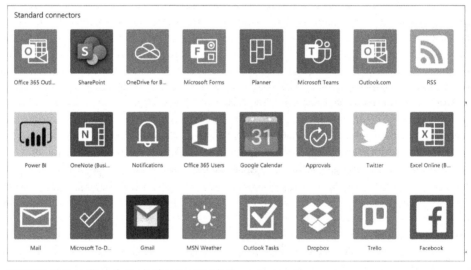

FIGURE 2-18 Sampling of standard connectors in Power Automate

The connectors designated as premium are available to licensed users of the standalone versions of Power Apps (both the per user and the per user, per app plans) and Power Automate (both the per user and per flow plans), as well as to Dynamics 365 users. The premium connectors feature those for many commercial Microsoft and third-party services, including SQL Server and Dynamics 365. A sampling of the premium connectors is shown in Figure 2-19.

Power Apps standalone licenses include Power Automate capabilities, as long as the Power Automate flows exist in the context of a Power Apps application. These contextual flows are permitted to use whatever standard and premium connectors are provided with the Power

Apps license. Standalone flows that are not part of a Power Apps application are not supported by the Power Apps license; a standalone Power Automate license is required.

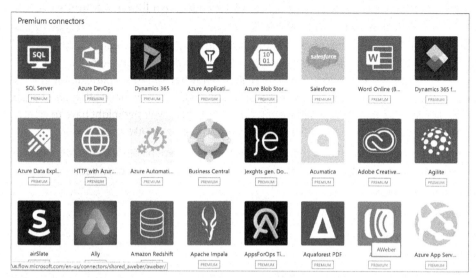

FIGURE 2-19 Sampling of premium connectors in Power Automate

Licensed Microsoft 365 and Office 365 users have access to the standard connectors in Power Apps and Power Automate, but they do not have access to premium connectors. To gain access to the premium connectors, they need a standalone Power Apps and/or Power Automate license as well.

EXAM TIP

Candidates for the PL-900 exam should be aware of the fact that, despite their being referred to by the single name Power Platform, the Power BI, Power Apps, Power Automate, and Power Virtual Agents tools are separate products, each requiring its own license and with its own licensing terms. For a full description of the licensing terms for Power Apps, Power Automate, and Power Virtual Agents, see the licensing guide available at https://go.microsoft.com/fwlink/?linkid=2085130.

Identify use cases for custom connectors

As mentioned earlier, a connector is a wrapper that surrounds a REST API supplied by the application or service that will be the data source. Power Platform provides connectors for a great many applications or services, but certainly not for every one. For developers who require access to data sources for which there are no public connectors available, it is possible for them to create their own custom connectors.

When a developer creates a custom connector, it is part of the current working environment and is usable only by the apps and flows operating in that same environment. It is also necessary for consumers running apps or flows that use custom connectors to have their own credentials for authentication to the data source, if the data source requires them. Unlike with public connectors, there is no way for consumers of a shared app or flow using custom connectors to inherit credentials supplied by the developer.

Depending on the application or service for which the developer will create a custom connector, there might or might not be an existing API with which the connector can communicate. A third-party application or service might already have an API in place. If not, the developer might have to discuss with the third party the possibility of their creating one. For an internally developed application or service without an API, the developer might have to create one using a tool such as Azure Functions, Azure Web Apps, or Azure API Apps.

There are several ways in which a custom connector can communicate with the API. When a developer runs the Custom Connector Wizard, the following options are provided:

- Create from blank
- Create from Azure service
- Import an OpenAPI file
- Import an OpenAPI from URL
- Import a Postman collection

OpenAPI (formerly known as Swagger) and Postman are definition file formats that provide the communication information the custom connector needs. When creating a custom connector from scratch (using the Create from blank option), the developer is led by the wizard through four stages:

1. *General*—Prompts for an icon and color for the connector tile and the host name for the API, as shown in Figure 2-20

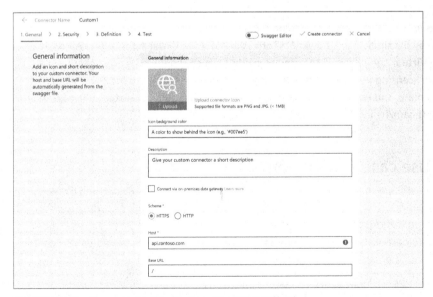

FIGURE 2-20 The General tab of the Custom Connector Wizard

2. *Security*—Prompts for the authentication method the connector should use to access the API: Basic authentication (as shown in Figure 2-21), API Key, or OAuth 2.0

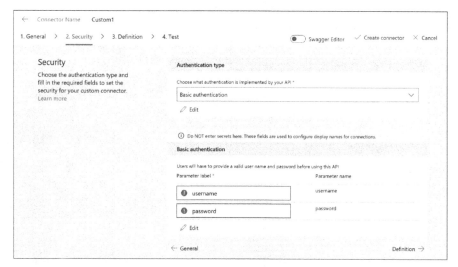

FIGURE 2-21 The Security tab of the Custom Connector Wizard

3. *Definition*—Provides the interface for creating the connector's actions, triggers, and policies, as shown in Figure 2-22

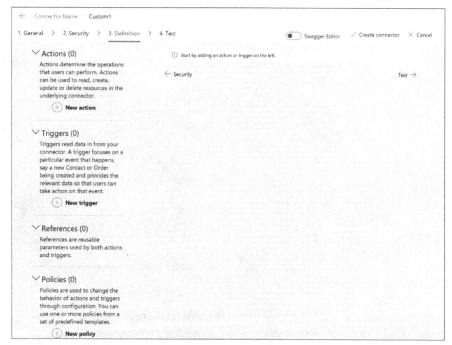

FIGURE 2-22 The Definition tab of the Custom Connector Wizard

4. *Test*—Provides a platform for testing specific operations in the custom connector, as shown in Figure 2-23

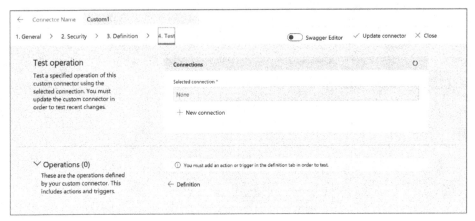

FIGURE 2-23 The Test tab of the Custom Connector Wizard

After developers have created custom connectors, they can share them with users inside their organization. Sharing an app or flow that uses a custom connector makes it accessible to the recipients of the share. Developers can also share their custom connectors with other users by selecting Invite other user from the Custom connectors page to display the interface shown in Figure 2-24.

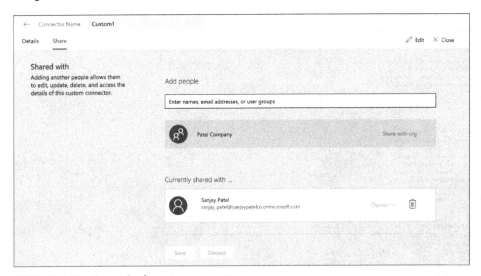

FIGURE 2-24 The Share tab of a custom connector

To share a custom connector with users outside of the organization, developers must submit it for certification by Microsoft, which validates the connector's functionality and content. The connector then undergoes a testing phase in a preview area, and when testing is complete, it is deployed for public access. Connectors that are certified and published by Microsoft must be released as open source software.

Chapter summary

- Microsoft Dataverse is a cloud-based data storage solution that the Power Platform applications can use to maintain their data in a secure, manageable environment.

- The Power Platform tools are able to connect directly to many different data sources, including local files, network resources, and cloud-based services.

- A default Microsoft Dataverse instance has a base set of standard tables, which the developer can populate with data from outside sources.

- Columns are the attributes within a table that contain specific types of data. If an entity in the Common Data Service is the equivalent of a table in Microsoft Dataverse, then a field is the equivalent of a column in the table.

- An environment is a container for the apps and flows created in Power Apps and Power Automate, as well as the data they use.

- Connectors are Power Platform components that allow Power Apps and Power Automate to interact with outside applications, services, and data files and utilize their data.

- Triggers are components in Power Automate that cause a flow to begin running. Actions are specific modifications made to the data provided by an outside application or service.

Thought experiment

In this thought experiment, demonstrate your skills and knowledge of the topics covered in this chapter. You can find answers to this thought experiment in the next section.

Ralph is studying for the PL-900 certification exam and becoming increasingly confused at the terminology surrounding Microsoft Dataverse. Some of the sources he is consulting have conflicting information, and he is not sure which sources are correct. Eventually, Ralph finds a source that explains how the terminology has changed in recent years. For each of the following Microsoft Dataverse terms, specify the letter of the earlier term it replaced.

1. Microsoft Dataverse
2. Table
3. Column
4. Record

a. Field
b. Row
c. Common Data Model
d. Entity
e. Common Data Service
f. Relationship

Thought experiment answers

This section contains the solution to the thought experiment. Each answer explains why the answer choice is correct.

1. e. Microsoft Dataverse was originally called the Common Data Service.

2. d. The tables found in a Microsoft Dataverse database instance were formerly called entities in the Common Data Service.

3. a. The columns found in a Microsoft Dataverse database instance were formerly called fields in the Common Data Service.

4. b. The rows found in a Microsoft Dataverse database instance were formerly called records in the Common Data Service.

CHAPTER 3

Describe the business value of Power BI

Microsoft Power BI is a cloud-based tool that allows users without coding skills or experience to create real-time graphical displays of data from a variety of sources and publish them to a cloud service that makes them accessible to virtually any desktop or mobile device. The objective of Power BI is to help users make their data more accessible by displaying it in graphs of various types, as shown in Figure 3-1, rather than as raw data. The designer of the display can thus interpret the data to highlight the information that is most important to the consumer.

FIGURE 3-1 A Power BI dashboard

Skills covered in this chapter:

- Skill 3.1: Identify common Power BI components
- Skill 3.2: Connect to and consume data
- Skill 3.3: Build a basic dashboard using Power BI

Skill 3.1: Identify common Power BI components

The process of creating a simple Power BI dashboard consists of the following basic steps:

1. Connect to data sources.
2. Transform the data.
3. Create report visualizations.
4. Build the dashboard.
5. Publish the dashboard.

As dashboard designers work through these steps, they encounter the various Power BI components that can aid them in creating a compelling dashboard design.

This skill covers how to:

- Identify and describe uses for visualization controls, including pie, bar, donut, and scatter plots and KPIs
- Describe the Power BI Desktop Reports, Data, and Model tabs
- Compare and contrast Power BI Desktop and Power BI service
- Compare and contrast dashboards, workspaces, and reports
- Describe the Power BI security model
- Describe using Power BI in mobile apps

Identify and describe uses for visualization controls, including pie, bar, donut, and scatter plots and KPIs

Visualizations are the formats designers can use to display data in a Power BI dashboard or report. Power BI provides a large selection of visualizations to choose from, including various types of charts, tables, maps, gauges, apps, and cards.

When creating a Power BI dashboard or report, the designer must first connect to a data source and, if necessary, transform the data. Once these tasks are done, the designer can select the visualization that Power BI will use to display the data from the Visualizations pane on the right side of the workspace, as shown in Figure 3-2.

Microsoft occasionally adds new visualizations to this pane, so it might not appear exactly as shown here. Some of the visualizations that are currently available for use include the following.

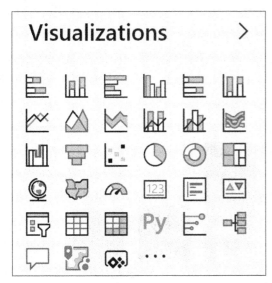

FIGURE 3-2 The Visualizations pane in the Power BI workspace

Bar and column charts

Bar and column charts display numerical values as adjacent horizontal or vertical shapes, making possible the easy comparison of relative values, as shown in Figure 3-3. Typically used for comparisons of like values, horizontal bars are preferable for qualitative values such as distance and speed. Vertical columns are commonly used for numerical values representing quantities, sizes, and costs. However, these definitions are not absolute.

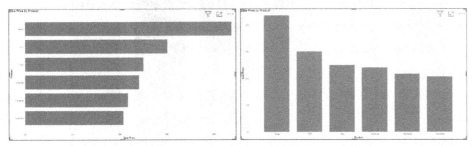

FIGURE 3-3 Bar and column charts in Power BI

Power BI provides visualizations supporting several different types of bar and column charts, including the following:

- *Stacked*—Charts that combine two or more values in each bar or column, as shown in Figure 3-4

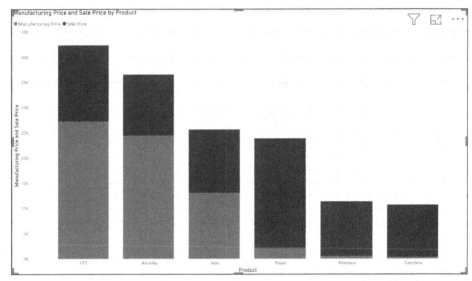

FIGURE 3-4 A stacked column chart in Power BI

- *100% stacked*—Charts that combine two or more percentages to display their values out of 100 percent, as shown in Figure 3-5

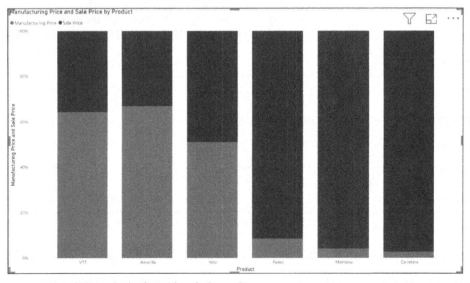

FIGURE 3-5 A 100% stacked column chart in Power BI

- *Clustered*—Charts that display groups of values as adjacent bars or columns, as shown in Figure 3-6

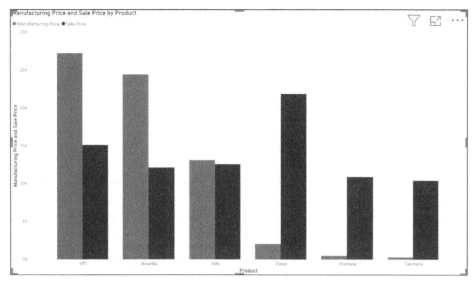

FIGURE 3-6 A clustered column chart in Power BI

- *Funnel*—Bar charts that display values in descending numerical order, creating a display that resembles a funnel, as shown in Figure 3-7

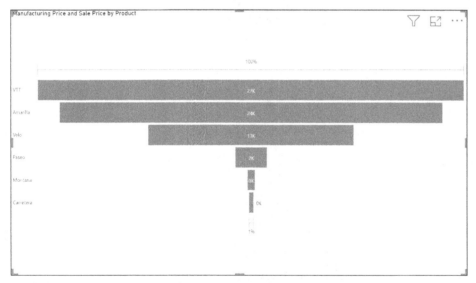

FIGURE 3-7 A funnel chart in Power BI

- *Waterfall*—Column charts that split a single statistic into sequential increments, typically representing intervals of time or category, as shown in Figure 3-8

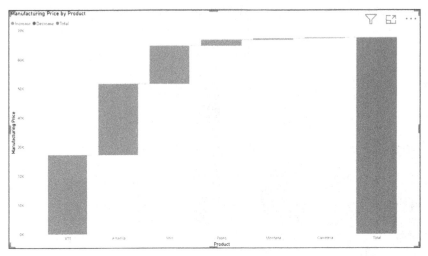

FIGURE 3-8 A waterfall chart in Power BI

Line charts

Line charts display one or more value sequences represented by horizontal lines running from each value to the next one, as shown in Figure 3-9. Commonly used for the presentation of values over time, as in financial profit and loss charts, the horizontal (or x-) axis traditionally represents the time interval, such as days, months, or years.

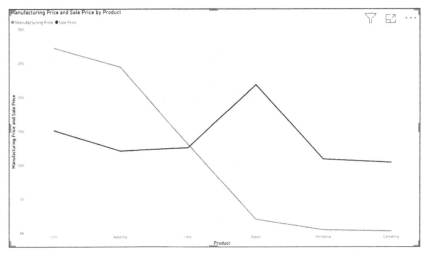

FIGURE 3-9 A line chart in Power BI

Combo charts

Power BI supports the combination of line and column charts into a composite that overlays line data onto a series of columns. The combination of the two chart types makes it possible to compare datasets that share the same x-axis, as in Figure 3-10. In this figure, the line represents the profit margin for a series of products and the columns represent their manufacturing and sales prices.

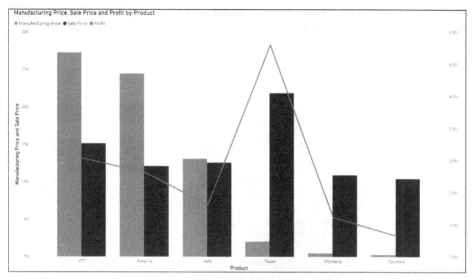

FIGURE 3-10 A combo chart in Power BI

Area charts

An area chart is essentially a line chart with the space between each line and the x-axis shaded, as shown in Figure 3-11. By using translucent shading, the chart can display the overlap between the two sets of values.

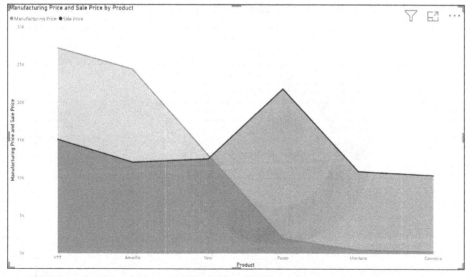

FIGURE 3-11 An area chart in Power BI

Pie charts

A pie chart consists of a circle resembling a pie divided into two or more slices that are shaded in different colors to represent numerical values, as shown in Figure 3-12. Designers typically use pie charts to illustrate percentages, with the entire pie representing 100 percent of the statistic.

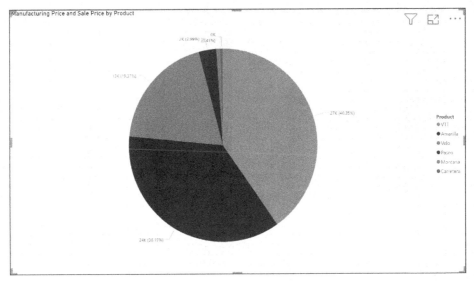

FIGURE 3-12 A pie chart in Power BI

Donut charts, a variation of the pie chart, consist of a ring (or annulus) divided into segments in the same way, as shown in Figure 3-13.

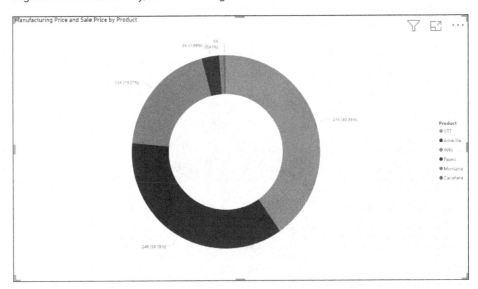

FIGURE 3-13 A donut chart in Power BI

Scatter plots

Unlike bar, column, and line charts, which usually dedicate the x-axis to a time scale, scatter charts (or scatter plots or dot plots) use both axes for numerical data values and indicate data points at the intersection of two values on the scale, as shown in Figure 3-14.

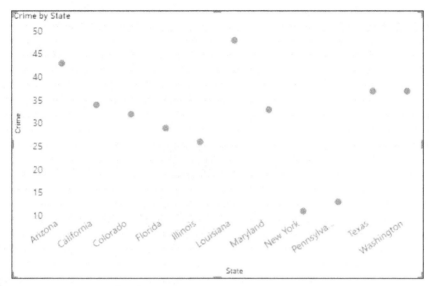

FIGURE 3-14 A scatter chart in Power BI

A variation on the scatter chart is the bubble chart, which adds a third data value by modifying the size of the data points to represent a third dimension, as shown in Figure 3-15.

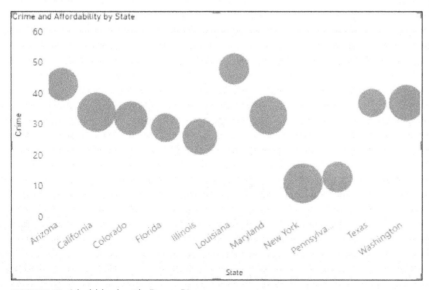

FIGURE 3-15 A bubble chart in Power BI

Key performance indicators

A key performance indicator (KPI) is a chart that indicates the progress of a single data point toward a specific predetermined goal. A KPI begins as a standard chart with a time interval on the x-axis, which represents the trend, and a data indicator value on the y-axis. Then the developer specifies a goal, which is a single value, and the chart appears as shown in Figure 3-16.

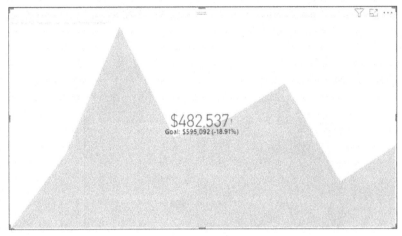

FIGURE 3-16 A key performance indicator chart in Power BI

The area chart in the background displays the current trend values, and in the foreground are the current numerical value and the goal value, plus a percentage that specifies how far off the current trend value is from the goal.

Cards

In a Power BI dashboard or report, a *card* is a tile that contains one or more numbers in large, easily readable type, as shown in Figure 3-17. Designers use a card when there is a single numerical value important enough to be displayed by itself.

FIGURE 3-17 A Power BI card

Gauge charts

A radial gauge chart displays a single value and its relationship to a specific goal, using a semicircular dial with a colored indicator representing the statistic's current value and a needle representing its ultimate goal, as shown in Figure 3-18, similar to that of an analog fuel gauge on an automobile dashboard.

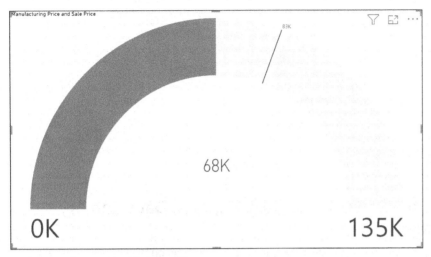

FIGURE 3-18 A gauge chart in Power BI

Key influencers

A key influencers tile allows consumers to explore the factors that affect a specific metric. When you create the visualization and select fields from the data source, Power BI performs an analysis and creates a chart like the one shown in Figure 3-19. Selecting one of the factors on the left modifies the column chart on the right.

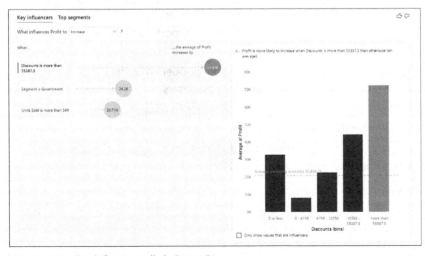

FIGURE 3-19 A key influencers tile in Power BI

Tables

In addition to the many types of charts and graphs available in Power BI, it is possible to include raw data in a dashboard or report in the form of a table, as shown in Figure 3-20.

Product	Manufacturing Price	Sale Price
VTT	27250	15106
Amarilla	24440	12096
Velo	13080	12561
Paseo	2020	21852
Montana	465	10890
Carretera	279	10395
Total	**67534**	**82900**

FIGURE 3-20 A table in Power BI

Describe the Power BI Desktop Reports, Data, and Model tabs

The Power BI service interface, shown in Figure 3-21, has a menu on the left side of the workspace that provides the primary means for users to navigate around the site. The collapsed menu icon (often called the hamburger button) at the top of the menu toggles between the full menu and a narrow button bar that clears more room for the workspace.

The tabs on the menu bar provide users with access to the various parts of the interface, as follows:

- *Home*—Displays tiles providing access to the user's favorite, frequently accessed, and recently accessed Power BI elements; the user's workspaces and apps; elements that have been shared with the user; and recommended apps

- *Create*—Provides users with guidance for creating a report using a published dataset or manually entered data

- *Browse*—Provides users with access to their recently-opened content, their favorite content, and the content shared with them by other users

- *Data hub*—Provides users with access to their published datasets and to the data published by other trusted users

- *Metrics*—Allows users to create scorecards that track the progress of chosen statistics towards specific goals, as shown in Figure 3-22

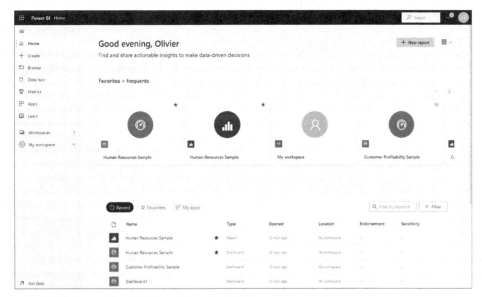

FIGURE 3-21 Home tab of the Power BI service interface

FIGURE 3-22 A Metrics sample in the Power BI service interface

- *Apps*—Displays tiles providing access to the apps the user has added to the interface
- *Learn*—Provides access to Power BI training, documentation, and community resources
- *Workspaces*—Displays a list of the workspaces created by the user
- *My workspace*—Displays a list of the elements in the user's current workspace, including dashboards, reports, apps, datasets, and local data sources

- *Get data*—Appearing at the bottom of the pane, displays the Get Data tab, with tiles that allow the user to discover and create content using files, databases, online services, and apps published by other users

In Power BI Desktop, when a user opens a file (or creates a new one), the navigation pane on the left contains the following tabs:

- *Report*—Displays the pages of the current report file and the Visualizations and Filters panes, which developers use to create and modify those pages
- *Data*—Displays the contents of the document's data sources and the controls for adding measures and transformations
- *Model*—In a report with multiple data sources, displays the relationships among the selected tables

The Report view in Power BI Desktop, shown in Figure 3-23, is similar to the workspace edit view in the Power BI service, with the Fields, Visualizations, and Filters panes on the right side of the screen, each of which the user can collapse independently for more workspace. However, Power BI Desktop has a ribbon at the top of the screen, much like an Office application, rather than the button bar found in the service.

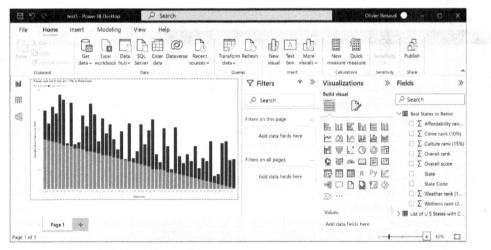

FIGURE 3-23 Power BI Desktop Report view

The Data view, shown in Figure 3-24, displays the currently loaded dataset in tabular form, allowing the user to examine the raw data, as opposed to viewing it in a visualization.

The Model view, as shown in Figure 3-25, displays all of the tables and columns in the currently loaded datasets, as well as the relationships between them. The lines connecting the tables indicate whether the relationship is one-to-one, one-to-many, many-to-one, or many-to-many.

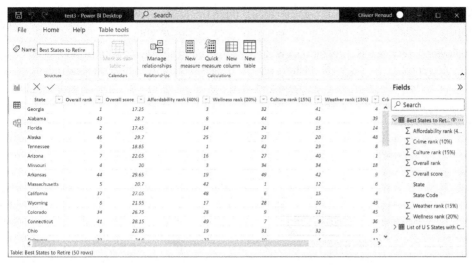

FIGURE 3-24 Power BI Desktop Data view

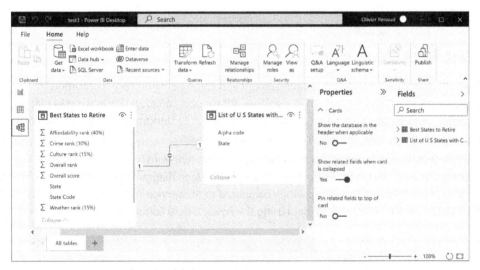

FIGURE 3-25 Power BI Desktop Model view

Compare and contrast Power BI Desktop and Power BI service

The Power BI service is the cloud-based environment that both developers and consumers use to create and access dashboards, reports, and other content. Power BI Desktop is a Windows application that provides more advanced data modeling and report development capabilities.

Because it is cloud based, the Power BI service is accessible to all users, on almost any device. Whatever tool developers use to create reports or dashboards, they publish them to the Power BI service so that consumers can access them freely. The Power BI service also allows developers to collaborate by providing them with access to documents stored in the cloud.

The Power BI service has a Reading view for consumers and an Edit view for developers. The Reading view displays the Pages and Filters pane, whereas switching to the Edit view moves the pages tabs to the bottom of the screen and adds the Visualizations and Fields panes on the right side, as shown in Figure 3-26.

FIGURE 3-26 Power BI service in Edit view

Power BI Desktop is intended as a development and editing environment; consumers cannot use it to access shared content. It also does not support collaboration in the way that the Power BI service does. There are no workspaces in Power BI Desktop; instead, users open individual content files that use a format with a .pbix extension.

The Power BI service and Desktop tools have some basic functions in common, but each has some capabilities that the other lacks, as shown in the Venn diagram in Figure 3-27. The primary strength of Power BI Desktop, when compared to the service, is the ability to access multiple data sources and model the data using the Power Query Editor tool.

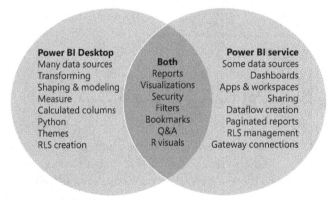

FIGURE 3-27 Power BI service and Desktop capabilities

Compare and contrast dashboards, workspaces, and reports

As noted in Chapter 1, "Describe the business value of Microsoft Power Platform," Power BI supports three types of distributable content: reports, dashboards, and apps. The report is the basic content unit, a multipage document that developers can use to publish large amounts of data in various formats. From a report, the developer can create dashboards, which are limited to a single page and consist of visual elements extracted from a report. An app is a means of packaging Power BI content from various sources for distribution as a freestanding unit.

When a user registers a Power BI account, the service creates a workspace for that user. A *workspace* is a private area of the service in which a user can work on their content prior to sharing it. A workspace can contain multiple Power BI elements, including datasets and Excel workbooks, as well as dashboards and reports, as shown in Figure 3-28.

FIGURE 3-28 A default workspace in the Power BI service

When the content is ready, the developer can then share individual elements or use the workspace as a container to create an app from its entire contents. Although it is possible for single developers to create Power BI dashboards and reports in their individual workspaces and then share them with consumers all over the network, Power BI can also be a collaborative development environment.

Users can create multiple workspaces in addition to the default one and provide other users with access to them. Using a shared workspace, a team of developers can work together to create Power BI content and keep it private until it is ready to share with consumers.

Power BI administrators control the ability to create new workspaces using the interface shown in Figure 3-29, found on the Tenant settings page in the Power BI admin portal. Administrators can grant the permission to everyone, to specific groups, or to everyone except specific groups.

Workspace settings

◢ Create workspaces (new workspace experience)
  Unapplied changes

  Users in the organization can create app workspaces to collaborate on dashboards, reports, and other content. Even if this setting is disabled, an upgraded workspace will be created when a template app is installed.

  ⬤◯ Enabled

  ⓘ The permission to create workspaces in the new workspaces experience preview is currently controlled by the permission to create groups in Office 365. By clicking Apply, the values below will control which users can create workspaces in the new workspaces experience preview. Learn more.

  Apply to:
  ⦿ The entire organization
  ◯ Specific security groups

  ☐ Except specific security groups

  [Apply]   [Cancel]

FIGURE 3-29 The Workspace settings controls in the Power BI admin portal

Creating a new workspace

The Workspaces tab in the Power BI service interface includes a Create a workspace button that opens the dialog box shown in Figure 3-30. As noted, the new workspace is now the default, so the process of creating a workspace does not automatically create an Office 365 group.

Create a workspace

Workspace image
  示 Upload
  🗑 Delete

Workspace name
  [Name this workspace]

Description
  [Describe this workspace]

Learn more about workspace settings

Advanced ∧

Contact list
  ⦿ Workspace admins
  ◯ Specific users and groups

Workspace OneDrive
  [(Optional)]

  Save   [Cancel]

FIGURE 3-30 The new Create a workspace dialog box in the Power BI service

To control access to a new workspace after it is created, click the Access button to open the Access dialog box, as shown in Figure 3-31, in which you specify users and the workspace roles assigned to them.

FIGURE 3-31 The workspace Access dialog box in the Power BI service

Describe the Power BI security model

Power BI, as implemented in Microsoft Azure, is a service that consists of two clusters: the Web Front End (WFE) cluster and the Back-End cluster, as shown in Figure 3-32.

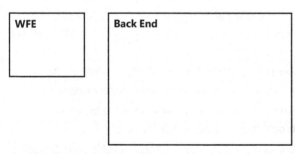

FIGURE 3-32 Power BI clusters architecture

The WFE cluster is responsible for the initial connection by users to the Power BI service and the authentication of the user account, in a process shown in Figure 3-33.

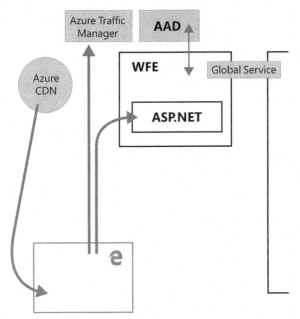

FIGURE 3-33 Browser interaction with the Power BI WFE cluster components

When a user directs a browser to Power BI by typing a URL or clicking a hyperlink, the following procedures occur:

1. The Azure Traffic Manager (ATM) examines the user's DNS record and directs the browser connection to the WFE cluster in the nearest Microsoft data center.

2. The WFE cluster directs the user connection to the Microsoft Online Services login page.

3. The user is asked to authenticate against their account in Azure Active Directory (AAD). When the authentication is successful, the login page directs the connection back to the WFE cluster.

4. The WFE cluster authorizes the user's Power BI service subscription with Azure Active Directory and, if the authorization is successful, obtains an AAD security token.

5. The WFE cluster consults the Power BI Global Service to determine the location of the correct Back-End cluster for the tenant to which the user belongs.

6. The WFE cluster directs the user connection to the correct Back-End cluster and supplies the user's browser with the AAD security token, the address of the Back-End cluster obtained from the Global Service, and information about the current session.

7. The user's browser connects to the WFE cluster and the Azure Content Delivery Network (CDN) and downloads the common files needed to interact with the Power BI service.

The browser maintains these files for the duration of the session with the Power BI service.

After the authentication and authorization processes are completed successfully by the WFE cluster and the browser downloads the necessary files, all subsequent Power BI communication takes place between the browser and the Back-End cluster directly, without further participation of the WFE cluster.

The Back-End cluster hosts a variety of roles, as well as the data storage media where the Power BI information is stored, as shown in Figure 3-34. The dotted line in the figure represents the division between the modules that are accessible to users via the public internet (on the left) and those that are accessible only indirectly (on the right).

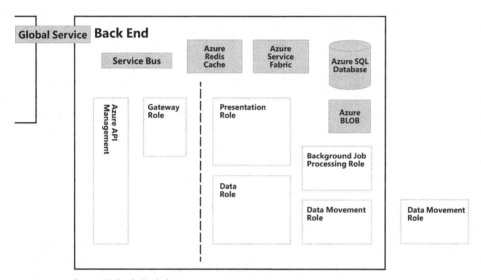

FIGURE 3-34 Power BI Back-End cluster components

The Back-End cluster is responsible for all the Power BI operations for authenticated clients, including the establishment and maintenance of data connections, the creation of the visualizations in dashboards and reports, and the storage of data. Users communicating with the Back-End cluster do so through the Gateway Role.

The Gateway Role and Azure API Management are the only modules accessible to users through the public internet. These modules accept and manage user connections, authorize users for specific content, and then relay all incoming user requests to the other modules in the cluster as needed. For example, a typical transaction in which a user attempts to access a Power BI dashboard, as shown in Figure 3-35, proceeds as follows:

1. The user's browser accesses the Power BI portal and connects to the WFE cluster.

2. The WFE cluster authenticates the user with Azure Active Directory (AAD) and authorizes the user's access to Power BI.

3. The browser connects to the Back-End cluster.

4. The user generates a request to display a dashboard and sends it to the Gateway Role in the Back-End cluster.

5. The Gateway Role forwards the request to the Presentation Role, which is responsible for supplying the data needed to create the visualization of the dashboard in the user's browser.

6. The Presentation Role sends the requested data to the Gateway Role.

7. The Gateway Role forwards the data to the user's browser, and the browser displays the requested dashboard.

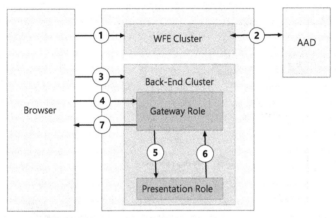

FIGURE 3-35 Power BI transaction

Thus, the Presentation Role (and all of the other non-public roles in the Back-End cluster, including the Data Role, the Background Job Processing Role, and the Data Movement Role) is protected from direct access through the internet by users, both authorized and unauthorized.

> ***NOTE*** **POWER BI PREMIUM**
>
> Power BI Premium is a subscription level that provides a tenant with a dedicated Back-End service cluster, as shown in Figure 3-36, created on virtual machines located in the same data center as the tenant.
>
> The Premium cluster contains separate instances of roles found in the Back-End cluster, including the Gateway Role, Azure API Management, Data Role, and Background Job Processing Role, as well as a separate Azure SQL Database. All communication with the dedicated Premium cluster goes through the shared Back-End cluster, which relays traffic to and from the Gateway Role in the Premium cluster.

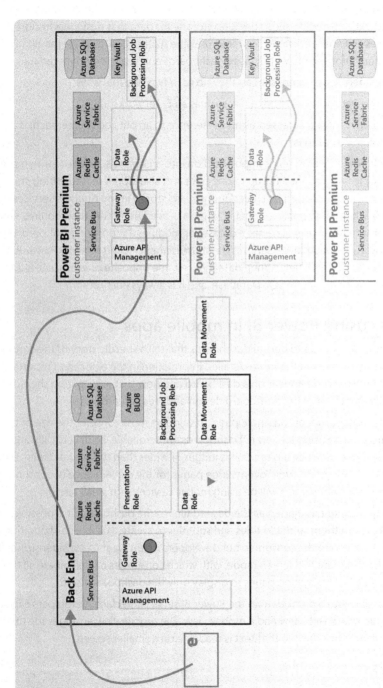

FIGURE 3-36 Power BI Premium Back-End cluster architecture

The Back-End cluster contains two forms of data storage: Azure Blob and an Azure SQL Database instance. Azure Blob is a storage solution that Azure uses for large amounts of unstructured data. Power BI uses Azure Blob storage for data that designers import from a source, such as an Excel worksheet. Power BI uses the Azure SQL Database for all other data, including tenant information, workspaces, dashboards and reports, and metadata.

When designers access data sources, they do so in two possible ways:

- *Import*—Data accessed from a file, such as an Excel worksheet
- *DirectQuery*—Data accessed using a reference to an outside source, such as a Share-Point site or a database

The Data Role in Power BI reads imported data into an Analysis Services in-memory database, in which it is retained for up to one hour and also stored in Azure Blob storage in encrypted form. Data accessed by DirectQuery is also stored in the Analysis Services database, but only while it is *in process*—that is, when a procedure occurs that requires access to the data, such as when a user accesses a dataset or modifies a report or dashboard, or when a data refresh occurs. The Analysis Services database is unencrypted to allow Power BI to access the necessary data immediately. When data is *at rest*, the opposite of *in process*, it is stored in either Azure Blob or the Azure SQL Database, and it is always encrypted.

Describe using Power BI in mobile apps

Power BI allows developers to design dashboards that tell a specific story to the consumers and provide them with access to the more detailed information in the associated reports. Deciding what information needs to appear on a dashboard and how that information should be visualized is an important part of the dashboard design and creation process.

Because a dashboard is only a single page, developers must consider the size of the screen that consumers will be using to view it. Dashboards are scrollable, both vertically and horizontally, so it is possible to create a page that is longer or wider than the actual screen, but developers typically should try to avoid overly large pages for the convenience of consumers. This is especially true when consumers will be using mobile devices with small screens.

After the developer has pinned all the desired tiles to the dashboard, it is possible to move them around, resize them, and add titles and subtitles to create a usable configuration. The choice of display is up to the consumer, but developers might want to consider sizing dashboards to accommodate full-screen mode, with which consumers can eliminate all the surrounding frames and navigation panes to display only the dashboard itself.

When working with a dashboard in the Power BI service interface, developers can switch between the standard web view and a mobile view. The mobile view arranges the titles vertically on a scrollable interface so that text is readable on a smaller screen.

Skill 3.2: Connect to and consume data

The first step in creating Power BI content is to access the data that the developer intends to illustrate using the charts and other types of visualizations that Power BI provides. Doing so calls for the developer to establish a connection to any of the data sources that Power BI supports and to select specific data provided by that source. Power BI Desktop allows developers to connect to multiple data sources and model the data into the form needed to tell an appropriate story in the Power BI report.

> **This skill covers how to:**
> - Connect to and combine data from multiple sources, including Microsoft Excel
> - Describe how to use Power Query to clean and transform data
> - Describe and implement aggregate functions
> - Identify available types of data sources, including Microsoft Excel
> - Describe use cases for shared datasets
> - Describe use cases for template apps
> - Describe options for viewing Power BI reports and dashboards

Connect to and combine data from multiple sources, including Microsoft Excel

The Power BI service allows developers to connect to any one of hundreds of data sources. However, in Power BI Desktop, it is possible to connect to multiple data sources at once and combine the information from them into a single data model.

As noted earlier in this chapter, connecting to a data source is the first step in creating a Power BI report. When you create a new file in Power BI Desktop, the startup screen includes a Get data button that starts the process of connecting to a data source by displaying the Get Data screen shown in Figure 3-37.

The developer can choose from hundreds of data sources, which generate proper screens for the submission of credentials. For example, to access data on a webpage, Power BI Desktop generates a From Web dialog box, as shown in Figure 3-38.

After the developer has connected to the data source, Power BI Desktop evaluates the data found at the source and displays the Navigator screen, as shown in Figure 3-39, containing all the tables it has found. Selecting a table and clicking Load adds the data to the Fields pane in the Report view.

FIGURE 3-37 The Get Data screen in Power BI Desktop

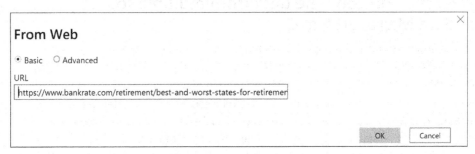

FIGURE 3-38 The From Web screen from Power BI Desktop

At this point, the developer can repeat the process to access one or more additional sources and add them to the Report view. In the Home tab in Power BI Desktop, the developer can select one of the icons in the Data group or select Transform data to open the Power Query Editor tool and select New Source.

Once the developer combines the queries, the data from the additional sources is added to the Fields pane, as shown in Figure 3-40. The developer can then proceed to use the data from the various sources to create visualizations for the report, but it is more likely that the data will require some modeling first. Developers do this using the Power Query Editor tool in Power BI Desktop.

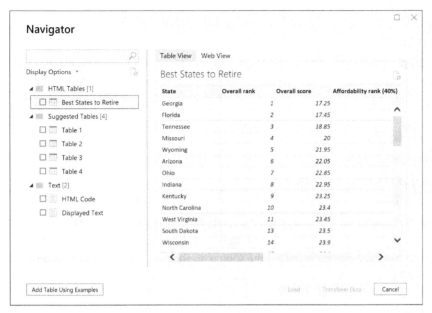

FIGURE 3-39 The Navigator screen in Power BI Desktop

FIGURE 3-40 The Fields pane in Power BI Desktop with two data sources

Describe how to use Power Query to clean and transform data

Whether a Power BI content developer accesses one data source or many, it is possible that the data might need modeling before it can be used effectively in a report. *Data modeling*—also called shaping or transforming data—is a term that can refer to a variety of tasks, including the following:

- Modifying data types
- Removing rows or columns
- Renaming tables, rows, or columns
- Splitting columns

The purpose of data modeling is to select and arrange the data accessed from the source so that it suits the visualization the developer intends to create. As always, modeling the data in Power BI does not change the original data in the source, so splitting, removing, and renaming rows and columns has no effect on the original data.

Modifying data types

One example of a data transformation is to modify the data type of a column. When a developer accesses a webpage as a data source, the resulting table might contain numerical values that Power BI Desktop sees as text. For example, the Overall rank column in Figure 3-41 is labeled as text (as shown by the ABC tag in the column header). Even though the values appear to be numbers, the Power Query Editor reads them as text and cannot use them in mathematical calculations.

FIGURE 3-41 Text column in Power Query Editor

By right-clicking the Overall rank column and selecting Change Type from the context menu, or by selecting the Data type drop-down list in the ribbon's Transform group, the developer can choose Whole Number to convert the column to numerical values that the Power Query Editor can use in mathematical operations (as shown by the 123 tag in the column header in Figure 3-42).

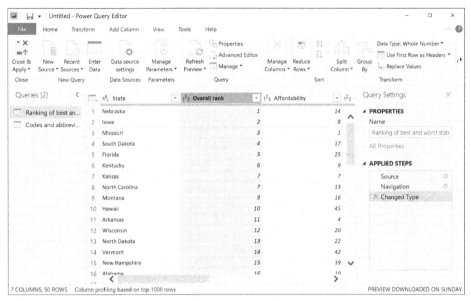

FIGURE 3-42 Whole number column in Power Query Editor

After the developer changes the data type, that modification appears in the Query Settings pane in the Applied Steps box as Changed Type. To undo the change, the developer can simply delete the Changed Type transformation. Each transformation a developer applies to the data is added to the Applied Steps list for later manipulation, if necessary.

> **NEED MORE REVIEW?** **USING POWER QUERY EDITOR**
>
> For more information on using the Power Query Editor, see https://docs.microsoft.com/en-us/power-query.

Removing rows and columns

When combining data from different sources, it is common for developers not to need everything that Power BI Desktop obtains from each source. For example, the Ranking of best and worst states for retirement webpage accessed in the previous section includes a column containing the names of the states. However, a developer might want to use the two-letter state abbreviations instead. To do this, the developer can access another data source that contains columns specifying the state names and their abbreviations. However, that data source might include other information as well.

For example, the data source shown in Figure 3-43 includes a column containing the full names of the states, as well as one containing the equivalent ANSI values, which are the standard two-letter state abbreviations. However, there are 11 columns in total, of which the developer needs only two. It is therefore possible to select the unneeded columns and select Manage Columns > Remove Columns in the ribbon to delete them.

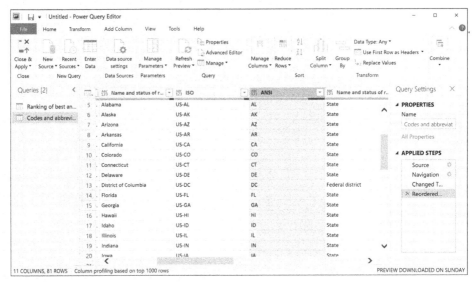

FIGURE 3-43 State abbreviations in a second data source

Renaming elements

Depending on the configuration of the data as it appeared in the source, it might be necessary for a developer to click the Use first row as headers command in the ribbon's Transform group to create column headers. It is also possible for the developer to right-click a column and rename the header to accommodate the needs of the other source to which the developer will merge or append the data.

Combining queries

Modeling data is essentially a matter of applying one or more queries to it. Power BI Desktop therefore refers to the modeled data from a source as a query. After the developer has modeled the data from multiple sources, it is possible to combine the queries in two ways:

- *Merge*—Adds columns from one data source to the existing columns from another source
- *Append*—Adds new rows from one data source to the existing rows in another source

In the previous example, the developer sought to add the state abbreviations to the Ranking of best and worst states for retirement data. To do this, the developer selects the target data source and, on the ribbon, selects Combine > Merge Queries.

In the Merge dialog box, shown in Figure 3-44, the developer selects the query to be merged and the columns to be matched during the process. In this example, selecting the State and State Name columns will synchronize the state abbreviations with the correct names.

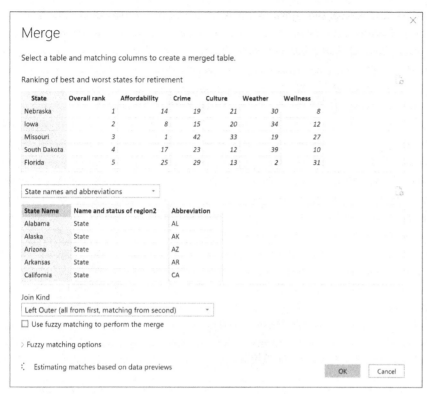

FIGURE 3-44 The Merge dialog box in Power BI Desktop

Clicking OK in the Merge dialog box causes the merged data to appear in the original source, as shown in Figure 3-45. The entire merged query appears as a single column with the word "table" in each cell, indicating that column contains all the merged columns in contracted form.

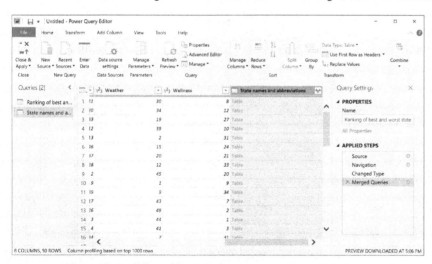

FIGURE 3-45 Power Query Editor with merged query

Clicking the Expand button at the right side of the column header displays the dialog box shown in Figure 3-46. By selecting or clearing check boxes, the developer can specify which expanded columns should appear in the merged query.

FIGURE 3-46 Expand dialog box in Power Query Editor

For this example, the developer should clear all but the Abbreviation check box and then click OK. The Abbreviation column is now merged into the Ranking of best and worst states for retirement query, as shown in Figure 3-47.

FIGURE 3-47 Power Query Editor with expanded merged query

When the data modeling process is complete, clicking Close & Apply in the ribbon's Close group adds the table from the Power Query Editor to the report in Power BI Desktop.

Describe and implement aggregate functions

Power BI uses the term *aggregate* to refer to mathematical functions that it executes on values obtained from data sources. When Power BI evaluates data, it automatically aggregates certain data types to anticipate the needs of the developer in creating a report. For example, when Power BI imports a table containing sales figures for a company's branch offices, it might aggregate those figures using the sum function to add up totals for the product sales categories. Although Power BI does this automatically, it is still possible for developers to modify the automatic aggregations or apply new aggregations to data as needed.

It is the Value element in a visualization that is typically aggregated by Power BI during its evaluation of the data. For example, in Figure 3-48, the values represented in the column chart are taken from the data source's Units Sold field. Hovering the mouse cursor over that field in the Value well indicates that the amounts used to create the chart are sums of the units sold. In the original source data, each product has dozens of Units Sold values for each product, broken down by country. Power BI has added the values for each product to arrive at the totals used for the chart.

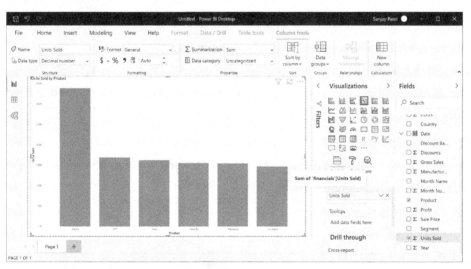

FIGURE 3-48 Power BI visualization with indication of aggregate

If for any reason a developer does not want to use sums of the units sold to create the visualization, it is possible to change the aggregate by right-clicking the field in the Value well to display the list of functions shown in Figure 3-49. For example, selecting Average instead of Sum causes Power BI to recalculate the values and redraw the chart with the averages instead of the sums. Other aggregates that Power BI supports include minimum, maximum, count (distinct), count, standard deviation, variance, and median.

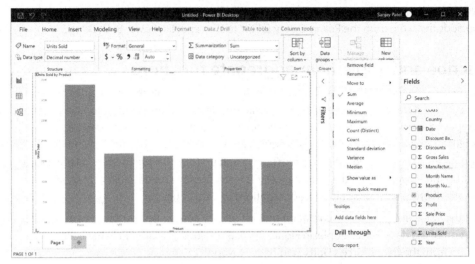

FIGURE 3-49 Power BI visualization with aggregate context menu

It is also possible to aggregate a text field, but Power BI obviously does not support mathematical functions such as sum and average for this purpose. Only functions such as count, distinct count, first, and last are applicable.

Identify available types of data sources, including Microsoft Excel

Before Power BI developers can do any modeling or visualizing, they must obtain the data they intend to use. The Power BI service and Power BI Desktop both provide support for hundreds of data sources, which they can access as local files, as databases within the organization, or as cloud-based services on the internet, whether public or private.

The data sources available in the Power BI service and Power BI Desktop differ, as does the means of accessing them. Microsoft is continually adding support for more data sources in Power BI, so it is common to see sources with beta or preview tags that are currently in development and might not be fully functional.

Power BI service data types

In the Power BI service, you can begin the process of selecting and connecting to data sources by clicking Get Data in the navigation pane on the left to display the screen shown in Figure 3-50.

The Get Data screen displays five tiles:

- *My organization*—Provides access to apps and organizational content packs published to the AppSource repository by other users in the organization

- *Services*—Provides access to apps and organizational content packs published to the AppSource repository by third-party users and organizations

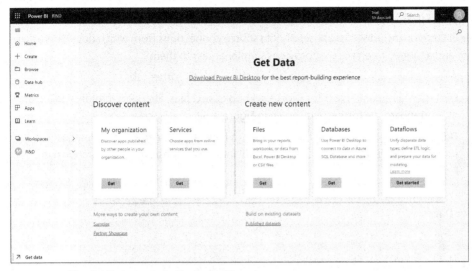

FIGURE 3-50 The Get Data screen in the Power BI service

- *Files*—Provides access to data files stored on the local computer or network, including Excel workbook files, comma-delimited value (CSV) files, and Power BI Desktop (PBIX) files
- *Databases*—Provides access to cloud-based databases, such as Azure SQL Database and SQL Server Analysis Services and on-premises databases
- *Dataflows*—Provides access to groups of tables that have already been transformed and prepared for use in visualizations

Some of the data sources listed in the Power BI service require developers to install and run Power BI desktop, as shown in Figure 3-51, which offers a more comprehensive set of sources.

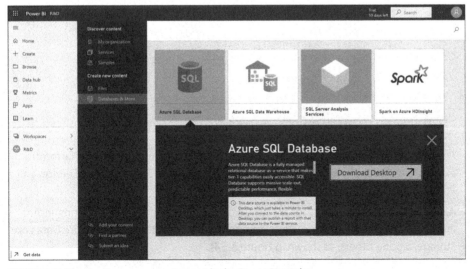

FIGURE 3-51 The Create new content screen in the Power BI service

Power BI Desktop data types

Power BI Desktop includes a larger set of data source connections from which developers can choose and a tabbed interface that provides simpler access to them:

- *All*—Contains a list of all the connections found on the other tabs
- *File*—Contains connectors for Excel workbooks, text files, SharePoint folders, PDFs, and other standard file formats, as shown in Figure 3-52
- *Database*—Contains connectors for many of the standard commercial database formats, including SQL, Access, Oracle, IBM Informix, Sybase, and SAP, as shown in Figure 3-53

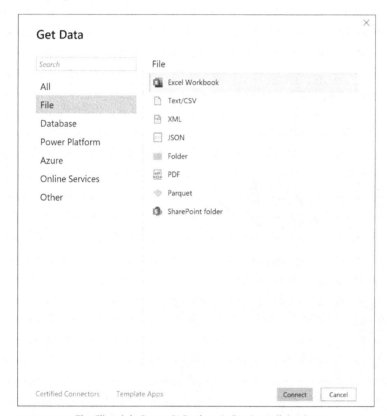

FIGURE 3-52 The File tab in Power BI Desktop's Get Data dialog box

- *Power Platform*—Contains connectors for data sources from other Power Platform elements, including Power BI datasets, Power BI dataflows, Common Data Service, and Power Platform dataflows
- *Azure*—Contains connectors for many Microsoft Azure data storage solutions, including Azure SQL Database, Azure Blob Storage, Azure Table Storage, and Azure Data Lake Storage, among others, as shown in Figure 3-54

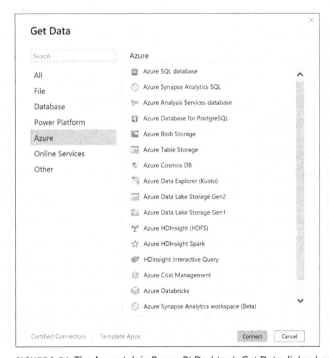

FIGURE 3-53 The Database tab in Power BI Desktop's Get Data dialog box

Get Data

Search

All
File
Database
Power Platform
Azure
Online Services
Other

Azure

- Azure SQL database
- Azure Synapse Analytics SQL
- Azure Analysis Services database
- Azure Database for PostgreSQL
- Azure Blob Storage
- Azure Table Storage
- Azure Cosmos DB
- Azure Data Explorer (Kusto)
- Azure Data Lake Storage Gen2
- Azure Data Lake Storage Gen1
- Azure HDInsight (HDFS)
- Azure HDInsight Spark
- HDInsight Interactive Query
- Azure Cost Management
- Azure Databricks
- Azure Synapse Analytics workspace (Beta)

Certified Connectors   Template Apps   Connect   Cancel

FIGURE 3-54 The Azure tab in Power BI Desktop's Get Data dialog box

- *Online Services*—Contains connectors for dozens of internet services, including Share-Point Online, Exchange Online, Google Analytics, Adobe Analytics, and many others, as shown in Figure 3-55

- *Other*—Contains connectors for various other sources, including websites, SharePoint lists, Active Directory, Spark, and Python scripts, among others, as shown in Figure 3-56

Depending on the nature of the connection, selecting one of the data sources generates additional screens with controls for making further file selections or supplying authentication credentials. When you create a dataset, the selections and credentials you specified with the data source are saved with it so that it will not be necessary to enter them again.

FIGURE 3-55 The Online Services tab in Power BI Desktop's Get Data dialog box

FIGURE 3-56 The Other tab in Power BI Desktop's Get Data dialog box

Describe use cases for shared datasets

Obtaining and modeling data are the first—and arguably the most important—parts of creating a report or dashboard in Power BI. These steps can be complicated and require a lot of time and effort, so Power BI makes it possible to share datasets with other users. This way, developers do not always need to have a complete understanding of the data they use to create reports, dashboards, and apps. They can access data that has already been transformed and modeled into a useful state.

Dataset sharing is an important element of the new workspace model in Power BI. Datasets saved to a new workspace are automatically shared with other new workspaces. For example, Figure 3-57 displays the Datasets + dataflows tab of a new workspace. The Customer Profitability Sample, Financial Sample, and Human Resources Sample datasets are stored in that workspace; however, the Retail Analysis Sample dataset is stored in another new workspace and yet it appears in this list.

This figure also includes datasets that have been endorsed to indicate that they are of particularly high quality and suitable for use by other developers. Datasets with the blue Promoted tag are endorsed by their creators. The green Certified tag appears on datasets that their creators have submitted for certification by a group of expert users selected by the organization's Power BI administrators.

FIGURE 3-57 The Datasets + dataflows tab of a new workspace in the Power BI service

It is also possible for developers to apply permissions to datasets to regulate what other users can do with them. When you select Manage permissions from the context menu of a dataset, its Manage access page appears, as shown in Figure 3-58.

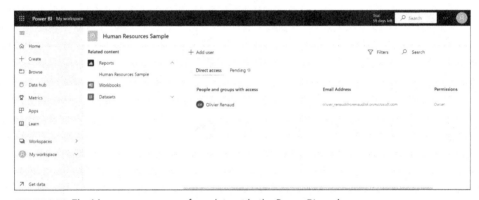

FIGURE 3-58 The Manage access page for a dataset in the Power BI service

From this page, the owner of a dataset can add users and assign them the following permissions:

- *Read*—Allows recipients of the permission to reshare the element
- *Build*—Allows recipients of the permission to build new content from the element

Describe use cases for template apps

Power BI template apps are sets of prepackaged reports and dashboards that users can download from the AppSource repository and connect to their own live data sources. Developers can create template apps and distribute them within their organizations or submit them for publication on AppSource.

On the Apps page in the Power BI service, clicking the Get apps button opens the AppSource interface, enabling the user to browse through the many templates available.

After the user selects and installs a template, Power BI creates a new workspace for it, and a Get started with your new app screen appears, as shown in Figure 3-59.

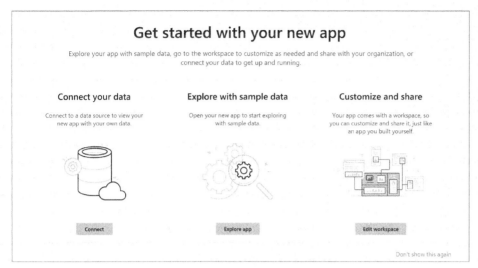

FIGURE 3-59 The Get started with your new app screen in the Power BI service

The Get started with your new app screen provides three ways to utilize the template app:

- *Connect*—Allows the users to connect the app to their own data sources, to create fully operational reports and/or dashboards using current data
- *Explore*—Provides access to the reports and/or dashboards in the app using sample data included with the template
- *Customize*—Opens the workspace created during the installation of the template, enabling the user to modify the reports and/or dashboards or just examine their construction

Describe options for viewing Power BI reports and dashboards

The basic data sharing paradigm of Power BI is for designers to create content and publish it to the Power BI service to share it with consumers. Designers can share content in a variety of ways, including the following:

- *Publishing*—Designers can publish reports and dashboards to the Power BI service and email links to consumers. When the consumer clicks the link and installs the content, it appears in the Shared With Me page in the Power BI interface.
- *Building apps*—Designers can package multiple reports and dashboards into an app and share it with consumers by installing the app in their workspaces, by sending them an installation link, or by posting the app on a website.
- *Exporting*—Designers and consumers can share Power BI content by printing from a report or dashboard and by exporting data to an Excel or CSV file or an entire report to a Power-Point or PDF file. Consumers can also store Power BI content on OneDrive for Business.

Interacting with Power BI content

After consumers have access to published Power BI content, they can interact with it in a variety of ways. For example, consumers can subscribe to dashboards and report pages using the interface shown in Figure 3-60, which causes Power BI to send a snapshot of the content to their mailboxes.

FIGURE 3-60 Power BI subscription interface

Consumers can also create alerts, using the interface shown in Figure 3-61, which cause Power BI to send an email when the value for a selected data point reaches a specified threshold.

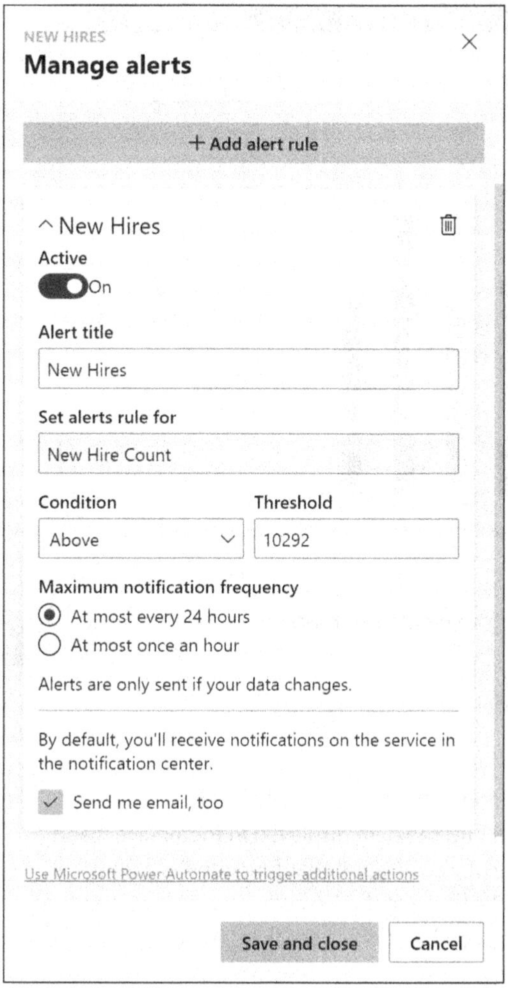

FIGURE 3-61 Power BI alert interface

Consumers can also exchange thoughts with colleagues by leaving comments in a dashboard or report, using the interface shown in Figure 3-62. The comments become part of the element, and other users can read and respond to them.

Using filters

Filters are a means by which Power BI designers and consumers can specify what data is displayed in reports (but not in dashboards, which do not support filtering). For example, if a dataset contains company financial information for 10 years, the report designer can create a filter that allows consumers to select specific years to be displayed in the report visualizations.

Any means by which data is categorized in a dataset can be used as a filter. If a company has five branch locations, as long as the dataset specifies a branch office for each data point, the report designer can use that information as a filter that allows consumers to select the branch office(s) to display in a report.

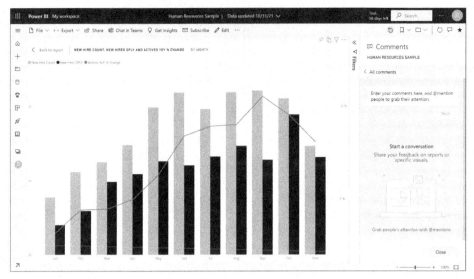

FIGURE 3-62 Power BI comment interface

There are four types of filters that designers can create in a report:

- *Report*—Applies to all the pages in the report
- *Page*—Applies to all the tiles on the current report page
- *Visual*—Applies to a single tile on a report page
- *Drillthrough*—Provides access to additional detail within a specific tile

Power BI reports support two means of selecting the data displayed in them: slicers and filters, as shown in Figure 3-63. A *slicer* is a type of visualization that functions as a filtering mechanism; it consists of a list of check boxes like those of the Executive slicer shown on the left side of the figure. Consumers can select any combination of check boxes to specify which executives should be represented in the report.

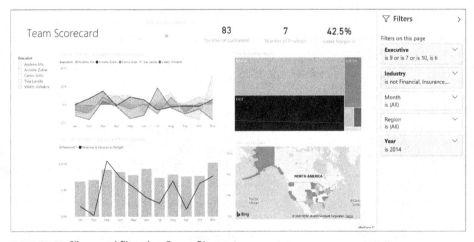

FIGURE 3-63 Slicers and filters in a Power BI report

The Filters pane, on the right side of the figure, contains the filters created by the report designer and the default filter values the designer specified. For example, there is a Year filter for which the designer selected the value 2014 as the default. However, the dataset contains data for other years, which the consumer can display by expanding the Year filter, as shown in Figure 3-64, and then selecting any or all of the other Year check boxes.

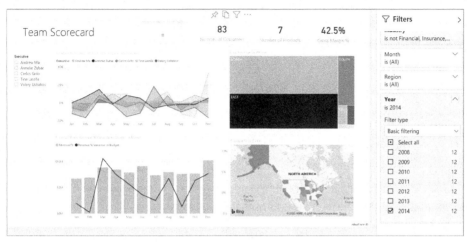

FIGURE 3-64 Power BI report with Year filter expanded

Power BI filters use basic filtering by default, but consumers can switch to an Advanced filtering option, shown in Figure 3-65, which allows the use of Boolean operators to create more complex filter behaviors.

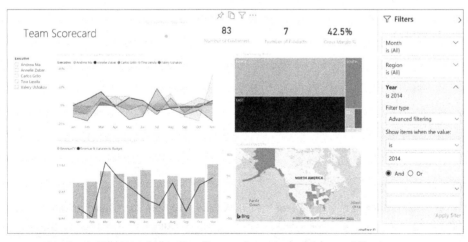

FIGURE 3-65 Power BI report with the Year filter configured to use Advanced filtering

When a consumer modifies the filters to display different information in a report, Power BI saves the changes made in that consumer's account only. When the consumer opens the same report again, even on another device, the changes appear as they were saved. The consumer can then use the Reset button at the upper right of the workspace to return all the filters to their default settings.

> **NOTE FILTER MODIFICATIONS**
>
> Consumers can modify the settings of a report's existing filters for use in the current or future sessions, but they cannot create new filters or delete existing ones. Filter setting modifications apply only to that consumer; they do not modify the appearance of the report to other consumers, and as always with Power BI, they do not modify the original data sources in any way.

In the Editing view used by report designers, the Filters pane contains three sections, as shown in Figure 3-66, which are labeled as follows:

- Filters on this visual
- Filters on this page
- Filters on all pages

The designer can drag data fields from the Fields pane to each section and then configure the filter for each field with the default settings that will appear to consumers.

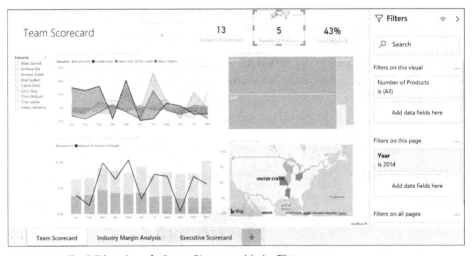

FIGURE 3-66 The Editing view of a Power BI report with the Filters pane

> **EXAM TIP**
>
> Power BI has introduced a new design for the Filters pane as of April 2020. Newly created dashboards and reports use the new design automatically. Existing dashboards and reports appear with the old design, in which the Filters controls appear in the Visualizations pane and provide the designer with the opportunity to upgrade to the new design. In the new design, a separate Filters pane adds new functionality, including the ability to format the Filters pane to match the report, hide all or part of the Filters pane from consumers, and lock specific filters so that consumers cannot modify them.

Skill 3.3: Build a basic dashboard using Power BI

A dashboard is a single-page Power BI document, like the one shown in Figure 3-67, that presents consumers with a selection of tiles containing highlights from one or more reports. The object of a dashboard is to tell a story relatively concisely, in relation to a report. It is assumed that if the consumers require more information, they can simply look at the report(s) from which the dashboard tiles came.

> **This skill covers how to:**
> - Create a Power BI report
> - Create a Power BI dashboard
> - Publish and share reports and dashboards

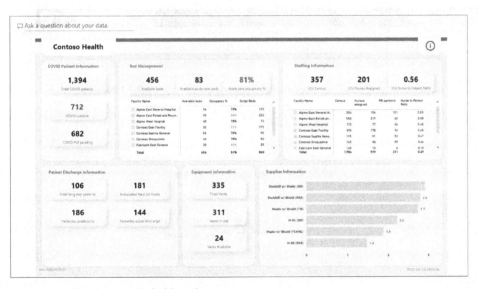

FIGURE 3-67 Sample Power BI dashboard

Create a Power BI report

At its simplest, the process of creating a new report in the Power BI service consists of the following steps:

1. Connect to a data source.
2. Create a new report.
3. Create visualizations.
4. Share the report.

While creating a basic report might be simple, each of these steps can be far more complex, depending on the nature of the data involved, how it is to be presented in the report, and who is permitted to access it. For example, the report might require data from multiple sources, and it might be necessary to model or transform the data before creating visualizations, and the report might require many pages with many visualizations.

For more complicated reports, developers might prefer to use Power BI Desktop instead of the Power BI service. As noted earlier in this chapter, Power BI Desktop provides access to more data source connectors, and it also includes the Power Query Editor, which provides extensive data modeling capabilities.

Creating a new report

Skill 3.2, earlier in this chapter, describes the various methods for connecting to a data source, modeling the resulting data, if necessary, and creating a dataset. With a dataset in place, the Create page in the Power BI service interface, as shown in Figure 3-68, provides a Pick a published dataset tile that provides the means to create a report from it.

FIGURE 3-68 Create screen in the Power BI service

Clicking the tile opens the Select a dataset to create a report dialog box, as shown in Figure 3-69. Then, choosing one of the available datasets and clicking the Auto-create report button generates the report document structure, as shown in Figure 3-70.

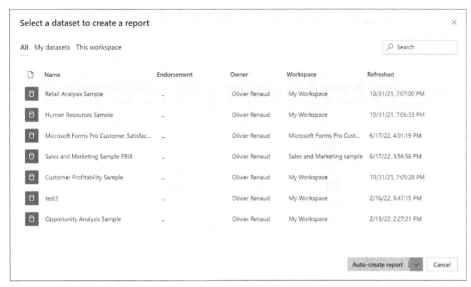

FIGURE 3-69 Select a dataset to create a report dialog box

FIGURE 3-70 Newly created report in the Power BI service

Creating visualizations

With the report structure in place, it is possible to create visualizations on the first page by selecting check boxes from the Fields pane and a chart type from the Visualizations pane. For example, selecting the Total Units Last Year and Total Units This Year check boxes in the This Year Sales category creates a simple column chart like the one shown in Figure 3-71.

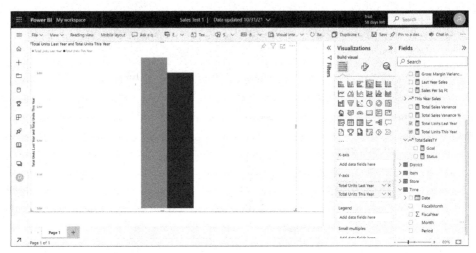

FIGURE 3-71 New visualization displaying the Total Units Last Year and Total Units This Year statistics

Then, selecting the Month check box in the Time category breaks the sales figures down by months and represents them as separate columns in the chart, as shown in Figure 3-72.

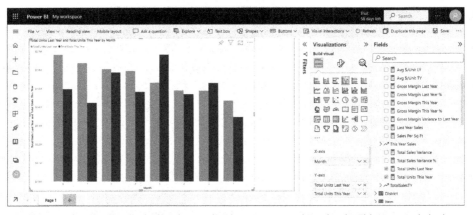

FIGURE 3-72 Visualization displaying the Total Units Last Year and Total Units This Year statistics by month

At the bottom of the Visualizations pane, the selected fields appear in the x-axis and y-axis areas. Developers can drag and drop fields to reorient the chart or drop additional fields directly into the Visualizations pane. Selecting a different chart icon in the Visualizations pane changes the chart type while leaving the field assignments intact, as shown in Figure 3-73.

This example displays one chart on the report page, but it is possible to resize the visualizations and create multiple tiles on a page. Developers can also create additional pages in the report by clicking the + (plus) button at the bottom left of the screen.

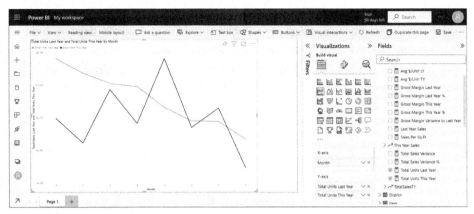

FIGURE 3-73 Visualization displaying the Total Units Last Year and Total Units This Year statistics by month as a line chart

Sharing a report

After creating a report and saving it to a workspace in the Power BI service, a developer can share it with other users by clicking the Share button in the workspace listing or in the open report to display the Send link dialog box, as shown in Figure 3-74.

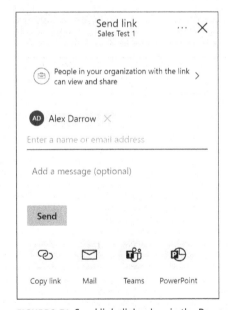

FIGURE 3-74 Send link dialog box in the Power BI service

Publishing a report

For developers working in Power BI Desktop, their completed content is not accessible to consumers until they publish it to the Power BI service, as in the following procedure:

1. With the completed content file open in Power BI Desktop, click the Publish button on the ribbon's Home tab or select File > Publish > Publish to Power BI. If the file has changes that have not been saved, a prompt appears to save it.

2. If the developer is not signed on to the Power BI service, a sign-on interface appears. After the sign-on is complete, the Publish to Power BI dialog box appears, as shown in Figure 3-75.

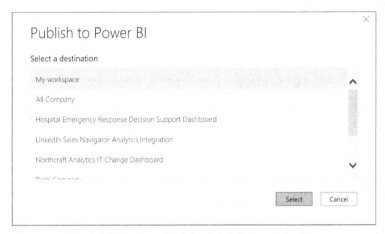

FIGURE 3-75 The Publish to Power BI dialog box in Power BI Desktop

3. Select one of the available workspaces listed in the dialog box and click Select.

4. When the publication process is completed, a Success message box appears, containing a link to the published file in the Power BI service, as shown in Figure 3-76.

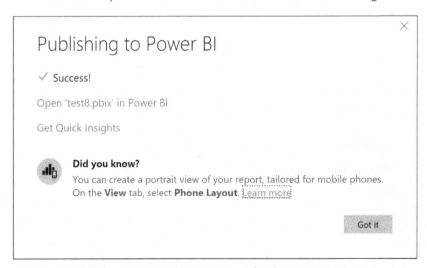

FIGURE 3-76 Publishing to Power BI Success message box in Power BI Desktop

Create a Power BI dashboard

A dashboard is a single page composed of *tiles*, rectangular placeholders containing visualizations taken from existing reports and datasets that update in real time. Dashboards are essentially gateways to the reports and datasets from which the tiles are taken. When consumers click a tile on a dashboard, they are taken to the report that is the source for the tile.

There are advantages to creating dashboards rather than having consumers themselves access the reports from which they were sourced. A dashboard is a single page, whereas a report can have many pages. Therefore, a well-designed dashboard contains only the information that is essential to the story that the developer wants to tell. Dashboards can also take their tiles from multiple dashboards and datasets. This allows a developer to use resources from several places to create a composite picture of a situation or process.

Although developers can create reports and datasets in either the Power BI service or Power BI Desktop, they can create dashboards only in the Power BI service. Therefore, any reports and datasets created and saved in Power BI Desktop must be published to the service before developers can use elements from them in dashboards.

The process of creating a dashboard begins with the creation of a report by connecting to a data source, modeling the data, and creating visualizations. There are then several ways to create a dashboard, but the simplest is to pin visualizations from the report to a new, empty dashboard, as in the following procedure.

1. Open a report in the Power BI service in Edit view and select a visualization. A toolbar appears in the upper-right corner, as shown in Figure 3-77.

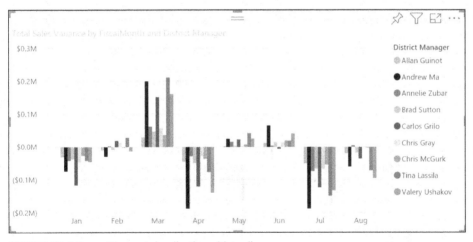

FIGURE 3-77 A Power BI report visualization with toolbar

2. Click the Pushpin icon in the toolbar to open the Pin to dashboard dialog box, as shown in Figure 3-78.

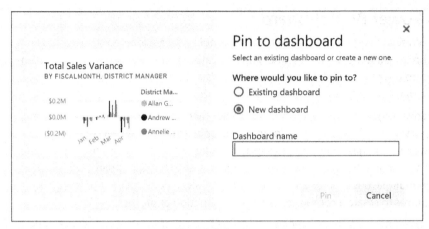

FIGURE 3-78 The Power BI Pin to dashboard dialog box

3. Select the New dashboard radio button, specify a name in the Dashboard name field, and click Pin. The new dashboard is created in the default workspace, and a Pinned to dashboard message appears.

4. Click Go to dashboard. The newly created dashboard appears with the selected visualization on it, as shown in Figure 3-79.

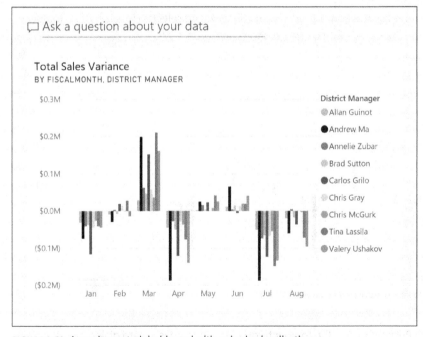

FIGURE 3-79 A newly created dashboard with a single visualization

After Power BI has created the new dashboard, the developer can pin additional visualizations to it, this time selecting the Existing dashboard option in the Pin to dashboard dialog box. The additional visualizations can come from the same report as the first one or from different reports.

If a developer wants to create a dashboard that consists of an entire page from a report, it is possible to do so without pinning each visualization individually by clicking the More options button on the page's toolbar and selecting Pin a live page from the context menu to generate a Pin to dashboard dialog box like the one shown earlier.

It is also possible to add tiles containing media content and other material directly to a dashboard by selecting Add tile from the More Options menu to display the Add tile dialog box shown in Figure 3-80.

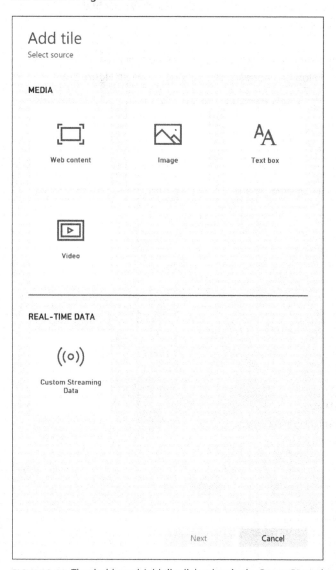

FIGURE 3-80 The dashboard Add tile dialog box in the Power BI service

Publish and share reports and dashboards

After creating a report or dashboard in the Power BI service, developers can share it with selected users. These users then become consumers of the content, meaning that they can view the material and interact with it (by adding comments, for example), but they cannot edit it.

EXAM TIP

To share content, both the developer and the consumer must have Power BI Pro licenses or be working in a Power BI Premium workspace. Candidates for the PL-900 exam can access the free version of Power BI, but to work with the sharing features, they can obtain a trial version of Power BI Pro from Microsoft.

When you select a dashboard or report in a service workspace and click the Share icon, the Share report or Share dashboard dialog box appears, like the one shown in Figure 3-81.

Share dashboard
ER2

Share   Access

Recipients will have the same access as you unless row-level security on the dataset further restricts them. Learn more

Grant access to

Enter email addresses

Include an optional message...

☑ Allow recipients to share your dashboard
☑ Allow recipients to build new content using the underlying datasets
☑ Send an email notification to recipients

Dashboard link ⓘ

https://app.powerbi.com/groups/689651f5-200e-40af-afe9-610a87510d23/dashl

Share   Cancel

FIGURE 3-81 The Share dashboard dialog box in the Power BI service

After specifying the addresses of the users with whom the developers want to share the content, they can select or deselect the following options:

- *Allow recipients to share your dashboard*—Allows recipients to reshare the content with other users

- *Allow recipients to build new content using the underlying datasets*—Allows recipients to utilize the datasets with which the dashboard was created, using the developer's credentials if necessary

- *Send an email notification to recipients*—Generates an email containing a link to the dashboard and sends it to each recipient

Chapter summary

- Visualizations are the formats designers can use to display data in a Power BI dashboard or report. Power BI provides a large selection of visualizations to choose from, including various types of charts, tables, maps, gauges, apps, and cards.

- The Power BI service interface has a menu on the left side of the workspace that provides the primary means for users to navigate around the site.

- When a user registers a Power BI account, the service creates a workspace for that user. A workspace is a private area of the service in which users can work on their content prior to sharing it.

- The Power BI service is the cloud-based environment that both developers and consumers use to create and access dashboards, reports, and other content. Power BI Desktop is a Windows application that provides more advanced data modeling and report development capabilities.

- The Power BI service allows developers to connect to any one of hundreds of data sources. However, in Power BI Desktop, it is possible to connect to multiple data sources at once and combine the information from them into a single data model.

- *Data modeling* is a term that can refer to a variety of tasks, including modifying data types; removing rows or columns; and renaming tables, rows, or columns.

- Power BI uses the term *aggregate* to refer to mathematical functions that it executes on values obtained from data sources.

- Power BI makes it possible to share datasets with other users, so developers do not always need to have a complete understanding of the data they use to create reports, dashboards, and apps.

- A dashboard is a single page composed of tiles, rectangular placeholders containing visualizations taken from existing reports and datasets that update in real time.

- After creating a report or dashboard in the Power BI service, developers can share it with selected users.

- For developers working in Power BI Desktop, their completed content is not accessible to consumers until they publish it to the Power BI service.

Thought experiment

In this thought experiment, demonstrate your skills and knowledge of the topics covered in this chapter. You can find answers to this thought experiment in the next section.

Ralph is new to Power BI, and he wants to create a dashboard that compares the number of COVID-19 cases in each of a selected group of East Coast US states on a particular day. He has found a website with a table containing the necessary data for all 50 states, which is updated daily. After studying Power BI for a while and planning the process of creating a dashboard, Ralph expects to perform the following tasks:

1. Create a dataset from the COVID-19 data on the website.

2. Create a report with table and column chart visualizations of the data for the 50 states.

3. Create a dashboard, and pin the table and column chart visualizations from the report to it.

4. Use filters to restrict the data in the two visualizations to the desired East Coast states.

5. Share the dashboard with selected users on the network.

However, Ralph is somewhat confused about whether to use the Power BI service or Power BI Desktop to perform these tasks. For each of these tasks, specify whether Ralph can use the Power BI service only, Power BI Desktop only, or either the Power BI service or Power BI Desktop. Explain your answers by specifying any additional tasks that Ralph might have to perform.

Thought experiment answers

1. To create a dataset from the website, Ralph must use Power BI Desktop only.

2. To create a report with the desired visualizations, Ralph can conceivably use either the Power BI service or Power BI Desktop. To use the Power BI service for this task, however, Ralph must first save the data as a PBIX file in Power BI Desktop and publish the file to a workspace in the Power BI service.

3. To create a dashboard, Ralph must use the Power BI service. If he has not done so already, he must save the report containing the dataset he created in Power BI Desktop as a PBIX file and publish it to his workspace in the Power BI service.

4. To use filters to limit the states displayed in the visualizations, Ralph can conceivably use either the Power BI service or Power BI Desktop to edit the report. If he does this in the Power BI service, the filters will be applied automatically to the dashboard. If he wants to do this in Power BI Desktop, however, he will have to publish the filtered report to the Power BI service again.

5. To share the dashboard, Ralph must use the Power BI service.

CHAPTER 4

Demonstrate the capabilities of Power Apps

As with the other Power Platform tools, Power Apps is designed for citizen developers with little or no coding experience. The tool allows users to create cloud-based apps that range in capability from simple information-gathering tools to internet-facing data access solutions. Power Apps can access hundreds of public and private data sources, as well as Power Platform's own Microsoft Dataverse. Unlike Power BI, which is based primarily on read-only access to data sources, Power Apps can be fully interactive, building up databases and replacing paper-based processes with digital ones.

The fundamental philosophy behind Power Apps is to provide organizations with a development paradigm that allows manual business processes to be realized as digital, automated processes without the need for an extensive development budget or a large team of development engineers.

Many large organizations have hundreds or thousands of manual procedures in place, and realizing them as traditionally developed applications could require a huge, costly, and lengthy IT expansion. With a no-code development environment such as Power Apps, the personnel who will actually be using the apps can be responsible for designing and building them. Instead of outside developers having to familiarize themselves with the users' needs, the users can decide what they need and when they need it.

Skills covered in this chapter:

- Skill 4.1: Identify common Power Apps components
- Skill 4.2: Build a basic canvas app
- Skill 4.3: Build a basic model-driven app

Skill 4.1: Identify common Power Apps components

Power Apps allows developers to create three types of applications: canvas apps, model apps, and portal apps. The processes for creating these apps are similar, but their functions and the design properties available to the developer are different.

Describe the differences between canvas apps and model-driven apps

Power Apps supports two types of internal applications: canvas apps and model-driven apps. The two types are similar in many ways, but they differ primarily in the flexibility of their interfaces and in the nature of the data sources they use.

Canvas apps

The canvas app is the original application type supported by the Power Apps tool when it was released, in 2016. Rather than write code, developers can create canvas apps by dragging and dropping elements onto a blank canvas in Power Apps Studio, in much the same way as PowerPoint users design slides. The developers then link the app to one or more data sources using the many connectors supplied with Power Platform and expressions that are similar to those used in Excel.

There are three ways to create a canvas app, as shown in Figure 4-1: by starting from a blank canvas, by starting with data from the Microsoft Dataverse or through one of the other Power Platform connectors, or by starting with one of the many templates included in the Power Apps portal.

FIGURE 4-1 The Create page of the Power Apps portal

In the sample help desk canvas app shown in Figure 4-2, the center pane displays the Login screen, the first one that users and admins will see when they open the app. The right pane contains controls for manipulating the appearance of the Login screen, and the left pane contains an expandable list of the various screens in the app and the components the developer has placed on them.

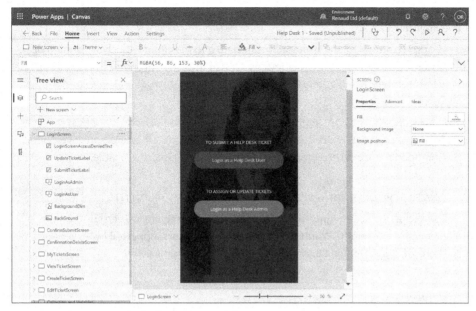

FIGURE 4-2 A canvas app in the Power App portal

This sample app has several other screens, some of which are shown in Figure 4-3. Developers can modify the screens as needed, both by adding or removing controls and by altering the colors and other cosmetic properties.

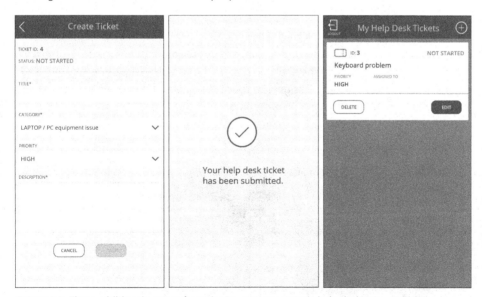

FIGURE 4-3 Three additional screens from the Power Apps sample help desk app

Canvas apps (unlike model-driven apps) provide the developer with complete freedom over the creation of the application interface. In addition to cosmetic properties, developers can configure canvas apps to display data in different ways, or even create controls that allow users to sort and limit the data.

After the app is completed, the developer can share it in the cloud with users running desktop browsers or iOS and Android mobile devices. One of the other strengths of canvas apps is their ability to be embedded in other services, including Power BI reports, SharePoint sites, and Microsoft Teams.

The help desk app shown in the earlier example uses a portrait orientation, which makes it suitable for display on mobile devices, such as smartphones and tablets. When developers build apps intended for use on browsers, landscape orientation is also available.

> **NOTE POWER APPS OPERATING SYSTEM AND BROWSER REQUIREMENTS**
>
> To run canvas apps, the Power Apps clients for mobile devices require iOS version 13 or later or Android 10 or later. PCs require Windows 10 or later. The browsers supported by Power Apps include Microsoft Edge, Google Chrome, Mozilla Firefox, and Apple Safari.

Model-driven apps

Compared with canvas apps, model-driven apps do not provide the same interface configuration capability. Instead, the developer begins by using business functions and processes to create a data model in the Microsoft Dataverse, and then they select and configure the components to be added to the app, such as forms, views, charts, and dashboards.

Power Apps currently has two interfaces available for the App Designer tool with which developers create and configure apps: modern and classic. The classic version of the App Designer tool is shown in Figure 4-4. As with canvas apps, model-driven app designs are based on components, but in the classic App Designer interface, the components do not resemble the elements as they will appear on the final app screens. Model-driven app screens are based on tiles, and developers use the App Designer to specify what tiles should appear, what data they contain, and how that data should be presented.

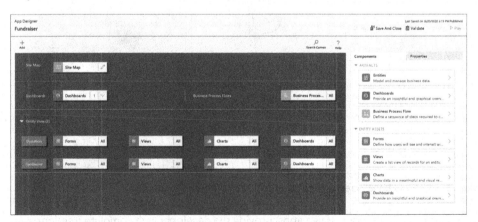

FIGURE 4-4 The classic App Designer interface in the Power Apps portal

The modern App Designer interface, shown in Figure 4-5, provides access to the same components used in the classic App Designer. However, the interface developers use to manipulate the components is different, and there is also a real-time WYSIWYG preview of the app screens as you work on them.

FIGURE 4-5 The modern App Designer interface in the Power Apps portal

EXAM TIP

As with several other Power Platform components, the transition between the modern and classic app designer interfaces is occurring gradually. At the time of this writing, the modern interface does not include all of the capabilities of the classic interface, so both are available for use. Eventually, the classic version will be eliminated entirely. PL-900 exam candidates should be familiar with the basic functionality of both interfaces while they are still available.

Using the source data and the components selected by the developer, the app then uses the Unified Client Interface (UCI) to design and create a tile-based display like the one shown in Figure 4-6. By rearranging the tiles, developers make it possible for the app to automatically adapt itself to the screen configurations of different device types. Canvas apps therefore have more design flexibility, but model-driven apps support more complex business logic. In some cases, a model-driven app can function as the back end for a canvas app.

Because they rely on the Microsoft Dataverse, model-driven apps have different licensing requirements than canvas apps. Microsoft 365 subscribers have the Power Apps/Power Automate license needed to create canvas apps using the standard set of connectors, but to use premium connectors or the Microsoft Dataverse, which is required for creating model-driven apps, an additional Power Apps license is needed.

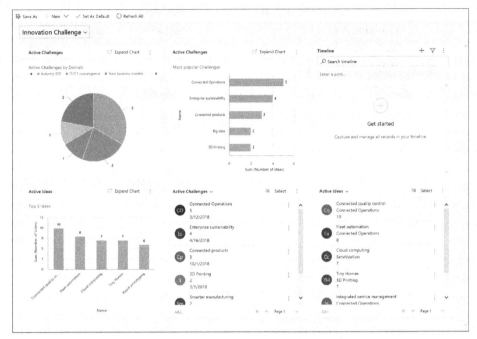

FIGURE 4-6 A model-driven app

Dynamics 365 is itself based on model-driven apps and the Microsoft Dataverse, so sub-scribers have the Power Apps/Power Automate licensing needed to create their own model-driven apps and use premium connectors. For users that do not subscribe to Microsoft 365 or Dynamics 365, there are standalone Power Apps licenses available on a "per user, per app" or "per app" basis, which include Power Automate capabilities. Both license options provide access to the full set of Power Apps capabilities, including the Microsoft Dataverse and stan-dard, premium, and custom connectors.

EXAM TIP

Candidates for the PL-900 exam should be aware that Microsoft provides time-limited trial versions of Microsoft 365 and Dynamics 365, which include the full Power Apps and Power Automate capabilities described here. A trial version of Power BI Pro is also available as a separate product.

Portal apps

A portal app is a means of providing users—both internal and external—with access to data stored in the Microsoft Dataverse using a website. Organizations can use portal apps to pro-vide customers, partners, and employees with self-service access to business information that eliminates the need for many call center and face-to-face transactions.

EXAM TIP

Candidates for the PL-900 exam should be aware that Microsoft and other sources use the word *portal* frequently and with many different definitions. In computing, the term *portal* is usually defined as a webpage that provides access to other services, applications, or websites. In the context of the Power Platform tools and other Microsoft cloud services, it is common to refer to their management and administration websites as portals. Be sure to avoid confusing these applications for the term with the portal app in Power Apps.

Portal apps were at one time a feature of a Dynamics 365 add-on product, but Microsoft later incorporated them into Power Apps. Users are limited to creating a single portal app in an environment. Because the portal app accesses and stores all of its data in the Microsoft Dataverse, there is no need or capacity for establishing connections to outside applications and services.

Selecting the Blank app tile and then the Blank website tile on the Create screen of the Power Apps portal prompts the user to confirm the provisioning of the current environment with the components needed to create the portal app. This can include the Microsoft Dataverse, if not installed already, appropriate tables and data, and a starter portal template. After the provisioning is complete, the portal app appears on the Apps page. Opening the portal app displays the starter page for the website, as shown in Figure 4-7. After the portal app has been created, the developer can then edit the website as needed by creating new pages, adding components, and applying templates.

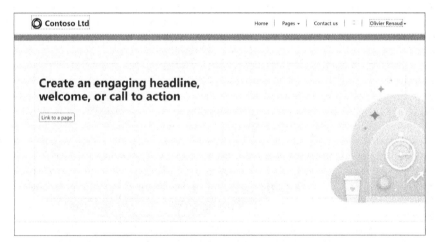

FIGURE 4-7 Starter page for a Power Apps portal app

EXAM TIP

As of this writing, the ability to create portal apps is still available in Power Apps. However, this feature has also been enhanced and packaged as a separate product called Microsoft Power Pages. Exam candidates should be conscious of the fact that portal apps have been removed from the PL-900 exam objectives.

Describe use cases for formulas

Formulas in Power Apps function in much the same way as formulas in Microsoft Excel. Developers can use formulas to perform operations on cell contents and to modify the functionality of controls, such as buttons, drop-down lists, and combo boxes.

Performing operations with formulas

For example, just as people can use the Sum function in Excel to total a column of cells, a developer can use the Sum function in a Power App to add the numerical values in multiple text boxes together. In Figure 4-8, the sample app shown has three text input controls—called TextInput1, TextInput2, and TextInput3—with numerical text in them. The fourth element is a label control with the following multifunction formula in it:

```
Sum(Value(TextInput1.Text),Value(TextInput2.Text),Value(TextInput3.Text))
```

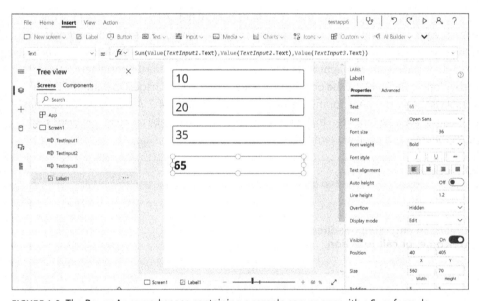

FIGURE 4-8 The Power Apps workspace containing a sample canvas app with a Sum formula

In this formula, the Value function converts the text in each of the first three controls into a value that can be manipulated. The Sum function then adds the three values together into a total that appears in the Label1 control. The developer can also elaborate on the formula by adding other functions, such as the If function in the following example:

```
If(Sum(Value(TextInput1.Text),Value(TextInput2.Text),Value(TextInput3.Text)) >=65,
"Pass","Fail")
```

This formula uses the If function to evaluate the sum, as in the case of a teacher calculating a quiz grade. If the value arrived at by the Sum function is greater than or equal to 65, then the Label1 control displays Pass, as shown in Figure 4-9; if the sum is less than 65, Fail appears.

FIGURE 4-9 The Power Apps workspace containing a sample canvas app with a formula using the If function to evaluate a sum

Configuring controls with formulas

Power Apps can also use formulas to configure controls. The Insert menu in the Power Apps workspace provides developers with a large collection of controls that they can add to canvas apps. After they are added, controls have properties that developers can configure using formulas. All controls have properties that define their appearance, such as their size, color, and location on the app screen. There are also properties specific to the function of the control.

For example, when a developer inserts the Date picker control into an app screen, as shown in Figure 4-10, the DefaultDate property shown in the drop-down list in the top-left quadrant of the app workspace has a default formula value of Today(), which appears on the app screen as today's date. The developer can change that default formula value to display any other date instead.

Selecting the Format property in the drop-down list displays a default formula value of DateTimeFormat.ShortDate, which causes the date to appear in the control using the format mm/dd/yyyy. As shown in Figure 4-11, developers can select that formula to display alternative values, such as ShortDateTime, which adds the time to the date, and ShortDateTime24, which adds the time using the 24-hour clock.

Scrolling through the list of other possible formula values, developers can also select Long-Date, which displays the date in the control as Friday, July 3, 2020.

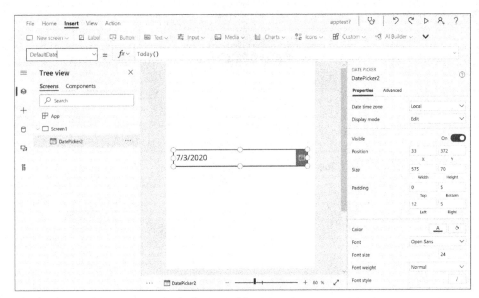

FIGURE 4-10 Configuring properties in the Date picker control

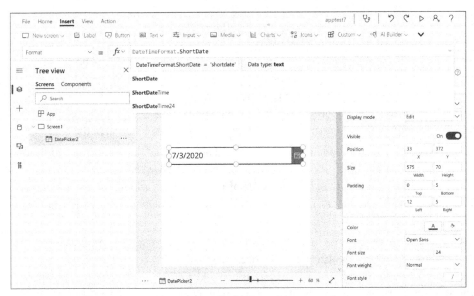

FIGURE 4-11 Configuring the Format property in the Date picker control

Skill 4.2: Build a basic canvas app

Canvas apps provide the developer with complete control over the formatting and appearance of the app. The process of building a canvas app involves connecting to a data source, placing controls on the app screens, and finally publishing and sharing the app to make it accessible to consumers.

This skill covers how to:

- Describe types of data sources
- Connect to data by using connectors
- Create an app from data
- Use controls to design the user experience
- Publish and share an app
- Describe embedding into Microsoft Teams

Describe types of data sources

Connecting to a data source is usually the first step in creating an app in Power Apps. This is true whether the app is built on the source data or the object of the app is to collect information from the consumers and save it.

An app can be based on data from any one of hundreds of data sources, accessed through the connectors supplied with Power Platform, a few of which are shown in Figure 4-12.

Organizations that subscribe to Microsoft 365 have access to cloud-based storage services that they can use as data sources, including OneDrive for Business and SharePoint. Both of these services can store files that contain the data on which an app is based. Dynamics 365 and Power Apps Pro subscribers have access to Microsoft Dataverse, which is a cloud-based database that apps can use to store the data they gather from users.

The many other connectors supplied with the Power Platform tools provide access to applications and services running on local servers and in the cloud. Power Platform has two classes of connectors, standard and premium, which are dependent on the Power Apps/Power Automate license used by the developers. The standard connectors provide access to most of the Microsoft cloud services, as well as to basic internet services and social media. The premium connectors allow apps to connect to higher-end commercial applications and services, including SQL Server, Dynamics 365, and various Azure services.

In some cases, a data source might just be a place to store data generated by the app, such as SharePoint or Microsoft Dataverse. In other cases, the connection might be the source for the data that is presented in the app, as in the Flooring Estimates sample app shown in Figure 4-13, which was generated from an Excel spreadsheet accessed from a OneDrive for Business connection.

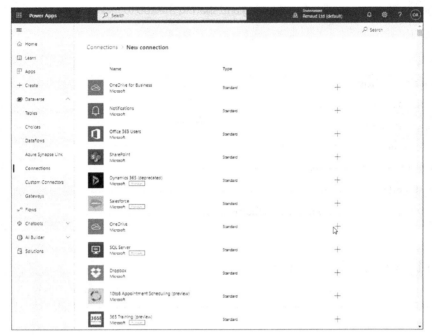

FIGURE 4-12 A sampling of connectors supplied with Power Platform

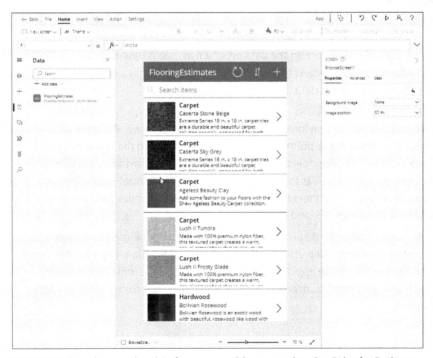

FIGURE 4-13 Sample app using data from a spreadsheet stored on OneDrive for Business

A spreadsheet is a type of table; this is the most common form of data used by apps in Power Apps. An app can read data from a table, modify the existing table data, and add new entries to a table. Other types of connections also can provide access to tabular data, such as SharePoint lists and SQL tables. Connectors can also access other types of data that are not tabular, such as calendars and email messages.

Connect to data by using connectors

Connecting to a data source is usually the first requirement in building a canvas app in Power Apps. How this happens depends on how the developer chooses to begin the build process. As noted elsewhere in this chapter, the Create page in the Power Apps portal provides three ways to create a canvas app:

- Start with a blank app
- Start with a data source
- Start from a template

Starting with a blank app

If a developer chooses to begin from scratch by selecting the Blank app tile on the Create page and then the Blank canvas app tile, the recommended first step is to navigate to the Data pane. Clicking Add data opens the Select a data source dialog box, which lists any current connections that are open, the Microsoft Dataverse tables that are available, if any, and all the available connectors, as shown in Figure 4-14.

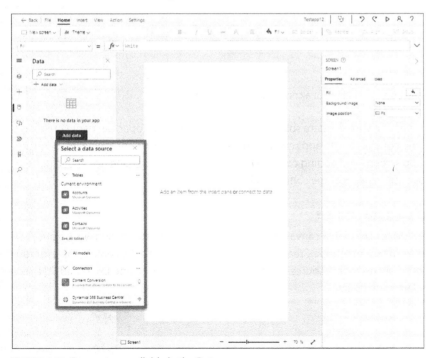

FIGURE 4-14 Connectors available in the Data sources pane

Depending on the nature of the connector, the developer selecting it will be presented with an interface providing access to the application or service. For example, if the developer selects the Import from Excel connector, a standard combo box appears, enabling the selection of an Excel file from a local or network drive. If the developer selects the connector for a subscription-based online service, a window appears, prompting for user account credentials, as shown in Figure 4-15.

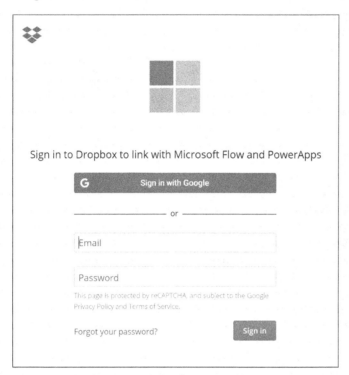

FIGURE 4-15 Sign-in pop-up window for a connector authentication

After the connection with the data source is established, the developer can begin building the app by adding controls to the app screens. There is nothing to prevent the developer from designing the app screens and adding controls before the data source connection is in place, but only the cosmetic aspects of the controls will function.

Starting with a data source

The second method for creating a canvas app is to start with a data source and work from there. The Start from section on the Create page, as shown in Figure 4-16, contains tiles for four of the most commonly used data sources: Microsoft Dataverse, SharePoint, Excel, and SQL, as well as a More data sources link.

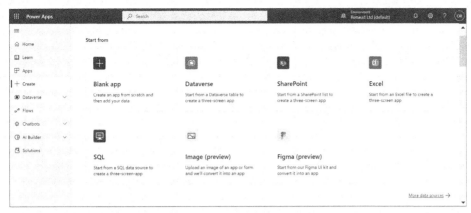

FIGURE 4-16 The Create page in the Power Apps portal

Selecting one of the tiles in the Start from section, such as the Excel tile, opens a Connections page, as shown in Figure 4-17. In this example, the Connections page indicates that there is already an open connection to the developer's OneDrive for Business account, where the desired Excel file is located. If there were no existing connection, the developer would have to click the +New connection button, select the OneDrive for Business connector, and type the necessary credentials to gain access to the data source.

FIGURE 4-17 The Connections page for a new app in the Power Apps portal

With the connection established, the developer can browse OneDrive for Business and select a data file containing tabular information that Power Apps can use. In this example, the chosen file is an Excel workbook containing the spreadsheet partially shown in Figure 4-18. Because an Excel workbook can contain multiple spreadsheets, a Choose a table pane appears, listing all the spreadsheets in the file for the developer's selection.

	Name	Category	Price	Image [image]	Overview
1					
2	Caserta Stone Beige	Carpet	$8.10	https://az787822.vo.msecnd.net/docume	Extreme Series 18 in. x 18 in. carpet tiles are a durable and beautiful carpet solution specially
3	Caserta Sky Grey	Carpet	$8.10	https://az787822.vo.msecnd.net/docume	Extreme Series 18 in. x 18 in. carpet tiles are a durable and beautiful carpet solution specially
4	Ageless Beauty Clay	Carpet	$1.98	https://az787822.vo.msecnd.net/docume	Add some fashion to your floors with the Shaw
5	Lush II Tundra	Carpet	$3.79	https://az787822.vo.msecnd.net/docume	Made with 100% premium nylon fiber, this textured carpet creates a warm, casual
6	Lush II Frosty Glade	Carpet	$3.79	https://az787822.vo.msecnd.net/docume	Made with 100% premium nylon fiber, this textured carpet creates a warm, casual
7	Bolivian Rosewood	Hardwood	$7.39	https://az787822.vo.msecnd.net/docume	Bolivian Rosewood is an exotic wood with beautiful, rosewood like wood with black
8	Golden Teak	Hardwood	$6.49	https://az787822.vo.msecnd.net/docume	The understated elegance of Golden Teak's creamy golden sapwood and unique dark-
9	Brazilian Koa	Hardwood	$5.69	https://az787822.vo.msecnd.net/docume	Its distinctive orange coloring and brown/black striping make it one of the most
10	Tobacco Road Acacia	Hardwood	$5.49	https://az787822.vo.msecnd.net/docume	As wood is a natural material, each board will vary in color or shade and provide you with a
11	Natural Hickory	Hardwood	$5.49	https://az787822.vo.msecnd.net/docume	Hickory is distinguished by its amazing color
12	Victoria Mahogany	Hardwood	$4.59	https://az787822.vo.msecnd.net/docume	As wood is a natural material, each board will vary in color or shade and provide you with a
13	Edimax Siaty Porcelain	Tile	$3.55	https://az787822.vo.msecnd.net/docume	Classic slate look Italian porcelain tile brought
14	Honey Onyx Marble	Tile	$8.99	https://az787822.vo.msecnd.net/docume	Honey Onyx is a beautiful beige brown onyx
15	Bianco Carrara Marble	Tile	$9.99	https://az787822.vo.msecnd.net/docume	A white marble from Carrara, Italy, in natural
16	Indian Autumn Slate	Tile	$2.99	https://az787822.vo.msecnd.net/docume	Millions of years ago, silt and mud from a river deposited soil at the mouth of a larger body of
17	Panaria Vitality Ceramic	Tile	$3.99	https://az787822.vo.msecnd.net/docume	Made of 100% eco-compatible content, slip &

FIGURE 4-18 Sample spreadsheet used to create app

After the developer selects a data file, Power Apps analyzes its contents and creates a working app that utilizes the data in an appropriate manner. In this example, Power Apps uses the spreadsheet information about types of flooring to create a catalog app that consists of the following three screens, as shown in Figure 4-19:

- A Browse screen listing all the flooring products
- A Detail screen for each product
- An Edit screen in which users can modify the information for a particular product

The design of this working app is based on the data supplied in the file and is basically Power Apps' guess of the developer's intentions. The developer can still modify the app in any way. In fact, if the supplied design is completely inadequate for the developer's needs, it might be easier to start over from scratch with a blank app and then connect to the data source.

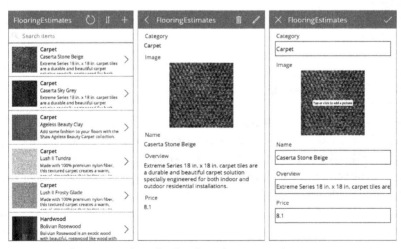

FIGURE 4-19 Three screens from the FlooringEstimates sample app

Starting with a template

As noted earlier, Power Apps includes a collection of templates that consist of app screen designs and data source connections intended to perform a specific task or solve a specific problem. This is a different approach to creating apps in that developers can attempt to locate a template that accommodates their needs as nearly as possible.

Templates perform two basic functions: they can serve as a blueprint for an app the developer actually needs, and they can be training aids, demonstrating how apps perform certain tasks. In many cases, the templates included with Power Apps include sample data and prompt the developer to supply a data storage connection such as OneDrive, as shown in Figure 4-20. The developer can then modify the app to use different text, source data, and images, as well as modify the controls and add or remove screens.

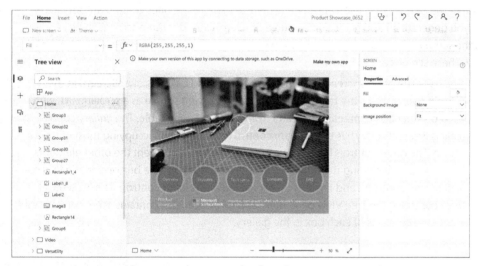

FIGURE 4-20 App created from a template prompting for a data storage connection

Create an app from data

With a connection to a data source in place, a developer can create a new app with controls that make use of that data. Power Apps supports the use of multiple data sources in a single app, which developers can use in various ways. When a developer uses a connector to access a resource, it is possible to access multiple tables or other elements. For example, in the sample app generated from an Excel spreadsheet shown earlier, it would be possible for the developer to connect to more than one table in the same Excel file. The initially generated app is created from a single table, but the developer can always add other tables later. In that case, each table would be considered a separate data source, even though they both use the same connection.

When apps are connected to multiple data sources, using one connection or more than one, the app can use them for incoming or outgoing data. An app can combine existing tables from multiple data sources, such as the product inventories from several branch stores, and combine them into a catalog app that provides a picture of the available inventory for the entire chain.

It is also possible to use multiple data source connections for different purposes. For example, an app can conceivably use one connection to retrieve data from a branch office in an Excel file, allow users to modify the data table in the app, and then use another connection to save the revised data to the environment's Microsoft Dataverse database in the cloud.

Use controls to design the user experience

With connections in place, the actual process of designing an app in Power Apps involves placing controls and other elements on the app screens to create a usable interface for the consumers who will be running it. The term *control* refers here to any of the display elements found on an app screen. The title box at the top of the screen, the buttons that trigger functions, and the panels containing data from your source are all examples of controls.

One of the best ways to learn about controls is to explore the ones created automatically when you generate an app from a data source or a template. The three screens shown earlier from the sample FlooringEstimates app are typical of an app generated from a tabular data source. These screens are as follows:

- *Gallery*—The gallery screen, shown in Figure 4-21 and called BrowseScreen1 in the sample app, displays the table data from the connected source as a scrolling list, with each product box containing the data from one row in the table. The *gallery* control (called BrowseGallery1) is the primary control for the screen, occupying most of its real estate. The other controls listed in the Tree View pane implement the other elements on the screen, including the title bar (called a *label* control), the buttons on the title bar (called *icon* controls), and the search box (called a *text input* control). The BrowseGallery1 control in the Tree View pane is expandable because it contains other controls that create the contents of each box in the gallery.

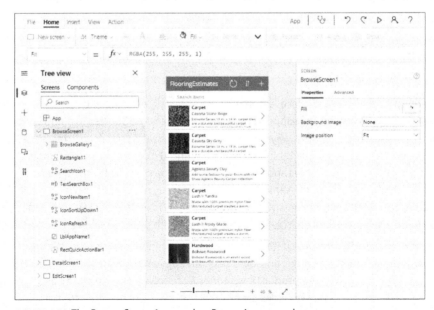

FIGURE 4-21 The BrowseScreen1 screen in a Power Apps sample app

- *Detail*—The detail screen, shown in Figure 4-22 and called DetailScreen1 in the sample app, displays all the information for one product selected from the gallery. Apart from the label and icon controls in the title bar, the screen consists mostly of *card* controls, which contain the individual data elements corresponding to the cells in the source spreadsheet.

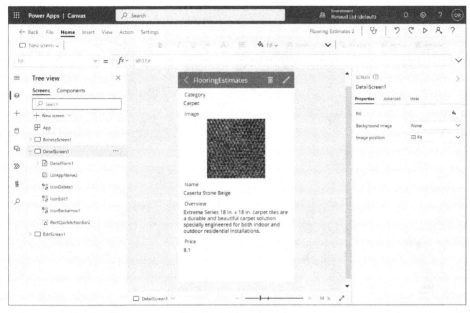

FIGURE 4-22 The DetailScreen1 screen in a Power Apps sample app

- *Edit*—The edit screen, shown in Figure 4-23 and called EditScreen1 in the sample app, displays the same information as the detail screen, but in editable controls so that the user can modify the information. Instead of simple card controls, which only display the data, this screen uses text input controls to contain the individual data points so that the user can modify them. All of these editable controls are part of an *edit form* control.

When working in the Power Apps Studio portal, clicking any element in a screen highlights the corresponding control in the Tree View pane and displays the properties of the control in the right pane. All controls have properties that specify how they look and what they do. The right pane in the Studio interface contains some of the properties for the selected control, using text boxes, buttons, and drop-down lists to allow the developer to modify the property values.

An equation bar near the top of the interface contains a drop-down list for selecting a property and an interactive function box, as shown in Figure 4-24, in which the developer can work with the individual property values. In the sample, the Data Source property of the EditForm1 control on the edit screen indicates that the data comes from the spreadsheet, identified as @FlooringEstimates.

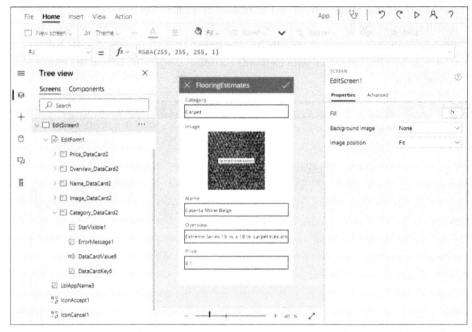

FIGURE 4-23 The Edit screen in a Power Apps sample app

FIGURE 4-24 The equation bar from the Power Apps Studio interface

This FlooringEstimates app contains only a small sampling of the controls available to developers in Power Apps and how they can make use of them. The insert bar, above the equation bar in the figure, contains buttons and drop-down menus that allow the developer to insert controls anywhere on an app screen. The buttons and menus include the following:

- *New screen*—Adds screens of various types to the bottom of the Tree View from a gallery of thumbnails, including list, form, email, and calendar formats

- *Label*—Adds a text box intended for display text

- *Button*—Adds a rectangular blue button that developers can resize and recolor as needed

- *Text*—Adds a box for the display and/or insertion of text in various formats, including plain text, HTML, rich text, and pen input

- *Input*—Adds controls that allow users to supply data, including text boxes, drop-down lists, combo boxes, date pickers, check boxes, radio buttons, and toggles

- *Media*—Adds controls that allow apps to display images, audio, and video, as well as accept user input from cameras and barcode scanners

- *Charts*—Adds controls that can display the source data as column, line, or pie charts, as well as insert Power BI tiles
- *Icons*—Adds controls that display small icons, such as plus signs, pencils, and check marks, which can function as buttons
- *Custom*—Allows developers to create, import, and export components
- *AI Builder*—Allows the insertion of standard AI Builder functions, such as the business card reader, the form processor, and the object detector

Publish and share an app

After developers finish building their apps, they have to save them and share them with the users who will access them. When a developer later makes changes to an existing shared app, the developer must publish the app so that the latest version is supplied to the users.

When a developer saves a canvas app for the first time, Power Apps opens a page that provides the option to save it to the cloud or to the local computer, as shown in Figure 4-25. After this first save, Power Apps automatically saves any changes made to the app every two minutes.

FIGURE 4-25 The Save as page in the Power Apps portal

After the app is successfully saved, the success screen includes a Share button. Clicking this opens the Share page, on which the developer can specify a user or group with which the app will be shared, as shown in Figure 4-26. By default, the accounts added on the Share page become users, who are permitted to run the app. Selecting the Co-owner check box grants the user the permissions needed to edit the app and share it with others.

FIGURE 4-26 The Share page in the Power Apps portal

After the app is saved, it is still possible for the developer or the co-owners to modify it, and Power Apps saves the changes every two minutes. However, it is necessary to publish the app to supply the sharing users with the latest version. Selecting Save from the File menu after making changes to an app produces a page with a Save button, and then another page with a Publish button. Clicking Publish causes the Publish pop-up shown in Figure 4-27 to appear.

FIGURE 4-27 The Publish pop-up in the Power Apps portal

Describe embedding into Microsoft Teams

In addition to publishing apps and sharing them directly with users, it is possible to integrate them into the Microsoft Teams environment. There are two ways of embedding Power Apps apps, as follows:

- *Tab app*—By embedding an app as a tab app, a new tab is added to a selected Teams channel. Clicking the plus sign in the row of tabs generates an Add a tab pop-up window in which the user can select the Power Apps icon, which opens a Power Apps pop-up containing a list of the available apps. Selecting an app causes it to appear as the new tab in the Teams channel.

- *Personal app*—Working from the Power Apps portal, users can choose an app and select Add to Teams from the More commands menu. After confirming the addition, the user opens Teams and a pop-up window appears with an Add button that allows the user to add the app to a team or to a chat.

Skill 4.3: Build a basic model-driven app

Rather than concentrating on interface design, as some developers tend to do when building canvas apps, model-driven apps are centered on the data they gather and present and the business processes they realize for users. Developers concentrate on what they want the app to do, rather than how it will look or function. Power Apps is responsible for the interface design.

This skill covers how to:

- Create a model-driven app from tables
- Modify forms
- Create and modify views and columns
- Publish and share an app

Create a model-driven app from tables

Model-driven apps have the same creation options as canvas apps. The Create page in the Power Apps portal contains a Model-driven app from blank tile as well as several model-driven templates.

Using the templates requires a Microsoft Dataverse database and the sample apps included with Power Apps. If the database and the samples do not exist in the current environment, Power Apps offers to create a new environment that includes both, as shown in Figure 4-28.

FIGURE 4-28 Power Apps model-driven app template message box

 EXAM TIP

Candidates for the PL-900 exam can install a trial version of Power Apps, as well as a trial version of Dynamics 365, to sample the full Power Apps experience. The trial versions are time-limited, and there is also a limit of one trial environment.

The real difference between building model-driven apps and canvas apps comes after the app is installed. As noted earlier in this chapter, there are currently two interfaces available for the App Designer tool: the modern and the classic. The modern interface displays a facsimile of the app screens, as shown in Figure 4-29, which the developer can populate by dragging and dropping WYSIWYG components.

FIGURE 4-29 The modern App Designer interface for a model-driven app

The classic App Designer interface uses a non-WYSIWYG workspace, like the one shown in Figure 4-30. The components are the same as those in the modern interface; they are just represented differently.

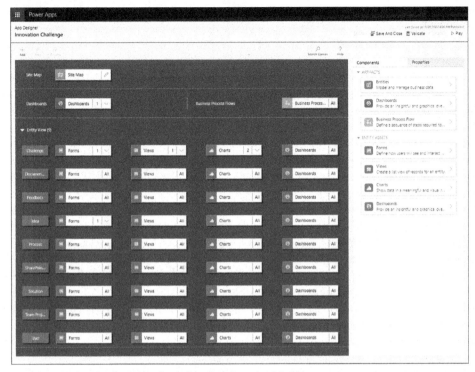

FIGURE 4-30 The classic App Designer interface for a model-driven app

Model-driven apps also differ from canvas apps in that they are always based on data accessed from Microsoft Dataverse. Developers design the app by adding tables from the database.

For example, in the Innovation Challenge app shown in the previous figure, the classic App Designer interface has nine rows in the Entity View section. The entities appear as buttons on the left side of the screen, and each entity has a row of four icon boxes representing the entity assets: Forms, Views, Charts, and Dashboards. These are the elements that determine what data will appear in the final app and how it will be presented.

EXAM TIP

As mentioned elsewhere in this book, Microsoft has changed the name of the Common Data Service to Microsoft Dataverse. The entities in the Common Data Service are now called tables, but in some Power Platform elements, the names have not been updated. The classic App Designer interface in Power Apps still refers to tables as entities, whereas the modern App Designer interface refers to them correctly as tables.

Developers can add entities to the app in the classic interface by clicking the Entities artifact on the Components tab and selecting from the list shown in Figure 4-31. Selecting a check box adds the entity to the Entity View area, creating a new row of assets for the developer to use.

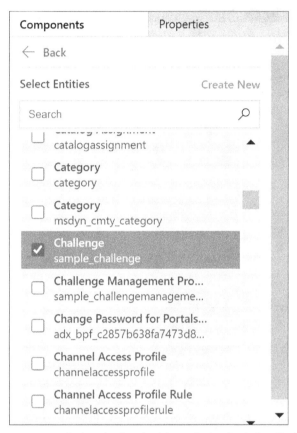

FIGURE 4-31 Entity selection check boxes in the classic App Designer interface

In the modern App Designer interface, developers can work with tables (instead of entities) and see the results of their modifications immediately. The tables available to the app are those found in the Microsoft Dataverse database for the selected environment. Developers can add to the capabilities of model-driven apps by adding tables to the database and populating them with attributes and records. Model-driven apps can also run users through business processes that create new records in specific tables and add data to them.

When a user runs the Innovation Challenge sample app, it appears as the dashboard shown in Figure 4-32. The table assets appear as tiles, which the app can shift around depending on the size of the screen displaying it. Developers do not choose a tablet or phone format in a model-driven app, as they do in a canvas app; the app itself controls the display.

FIGURE 4-32 The Innovation Challenge sample model-driven app

Modify forms

In the Innovation Challenge sample app, the first row of tiles in the dashboard, as shown in the previous figure, contains two charts called Active Challenges and a list called Active Ideas. The configuration of the table assets for Challenge and Idea rows in the App Designer is what makes the data from those tables appear as they do.

For example, in the classic App Designer interface for this app, the Challenge entity has a number 2 in its Charts asset box. Selecting that box displays the Select Charts interface in the Components pane, as shown in Figure 4-33. The two check boxes selected are Active Challenges by Domain and Most popular Challenges, which, not coincidentally, are the two charts that appear in the Innovation Challenge dashboard. The same chart names appear in the modern App Designer interface when displaying the Challenge view from the Pages pane, as shown in Figure 4-34.

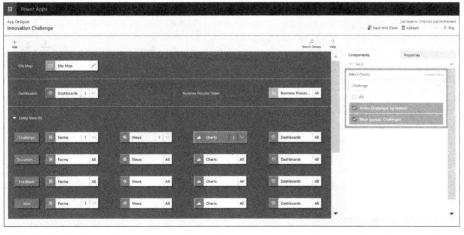

FIGURE 4-33 The Select Charts interface in the Components pane of the classic App Designer interface

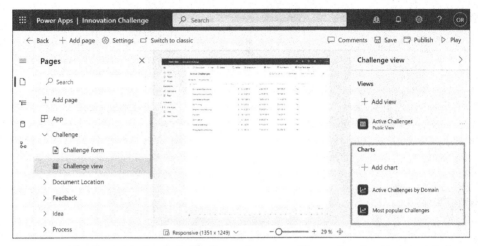

FIGURE 4-34 The Charts interface in the Challenge view pane of the modern App Designer interface

Clicking the down arrow in the classic App Designer interface's Charts asset box opens a drop-down list with the names of the two charts, each with an edit icon that opens the Chart Designer window, as shown in Figure 4-35. The modern App Designer interface provides access to the same Chart Designer window through the More Options menu for each chart name. In this window, the developer can change the appearance of the chart by selecting a chart type and configuring its properties.

FIGURE 4-35 The Power Apps Chart Designer interface

Forms appear in model-driven apps when users view table data in a table format and click the New button to create a new record in the table. For example, selecting the Challenges screen in the Innovation Challenge app and creating a new record displays the form shown in Figure 4-36, which is similar in appearance to a business process flow in Power Automate, taking the user through multiple stages, beginning with Setup, with several steps to complete in each stage.

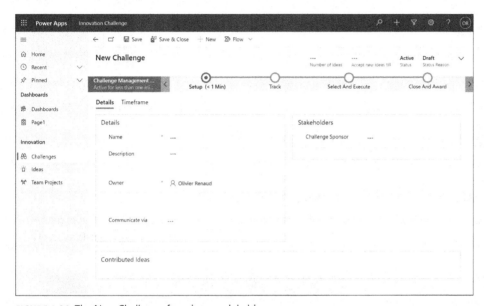

FIGURE 4-36 The New Challenge form in a model-driven app

Both of the App Designer interfaces allow developers to edit forms in the same way they edit charts. The Forms asset box in the classic App Designer interface provides an edit button for each of the forms appearing in the drop-down list, and in the modern interface, the forms have an Edit command in their More Options menus. These controls open the Form Editor interface, as shown in Figure 4-37. The Form Editor has a WYSIWYG display of the form in the center pane. In the left pane, the developer selects the fields that will appear in the form, and the right pane contains the configurable properties for the selected field. After modifying the form, the developer must save the changes and publish the form so that it can appear in the live app.

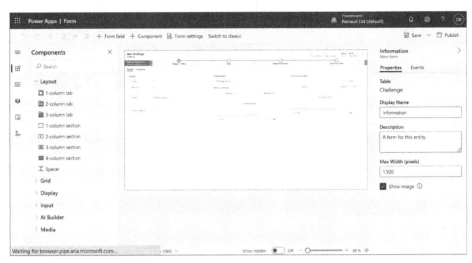

FIGURE 4-37 The Power Apps Form Editor interface

Create and modify views and columns

A view in a model-driven app is a display of information from the Microsoft Dataverse database in tabular form, as shown in Figure 4-38. Views can also appear on dashboards as scrollable lists, as shown earlier.

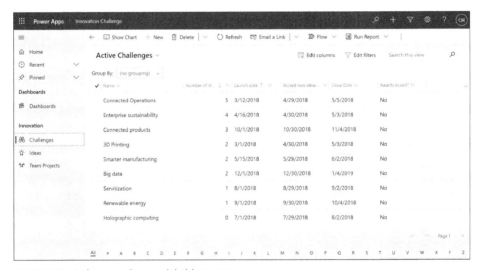

FIGURE 4-38 A view page in a model-driven app

Developers can modify views from the table asset boxes just as they can charts and forms. The View Editor interface, shown in Figure 4-39, is similar to the Form Editor, with selectable fields listed in the left pane, editable properties in the right pane, and a real-time display of the view in the center pane, to which the developer can add and remove columns.

FIGURE 4-39 The View Editor interface in a model-driven app

Publish and share an app

After working with a model-driven app, the developer must save the changes using the Save button in the upper-right corner of the App Designer interface. Saving the changes in the classic App Designer interface activates the Validate and Publish buttons. Validating the app checks the components for asset dependencies and any other issues that could affect their performance and displays error, warning, or information messages like those shown in Figure 4-40.

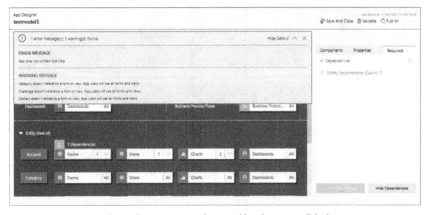

FIGURE 4-40 Error and warning messages detected by the app validation process

After addressing any problems with the app, the developer must click the Publish button. Doing so activates the Play button in both App Designer interfaces and also makes the updated version of the app available to Power Apps users.

For users to run model-driven apps, the developer must share the app with the individual users or a group to which the users belong. Security for model-driven apps is role based. Power Apps has predefined roles that might be appropriate for some apps, or the developer can create custom roles that contain the permissions needed to run an app.

To share an app in Power Apps, the developer selects the app and clicks the Share button to open the Share pop-up for that app. Selecting the app allows the developer to select the predefined standard roles to assign to users. Then, the developer supplies a user or group name in the People text box, chooses the correct user, and selects the role to assign to the user, as shown in Figure 4-41. If the predefined security roles are not appropriate for the app, the developer can click Manage security roles and create a new custom app.

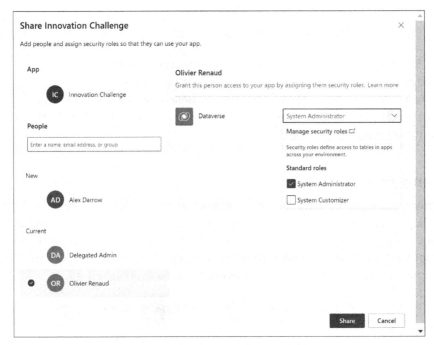

FIGURE 4-41 The Share pop-up interface for a specific model-driven app

Chapter summary

- Power Apps is designed for citizen developers with little or no coding experience.
- Developers create canvas apps by dragging and dropping elements onto screens in Power Apps Studio; model-driven apps do not provide the same interface configuration capability.

- A portal app is a means of providing users—both internal and external—with access to data stored in the Microsoft Dataverse using a website.

- The process of building a canvas app involves connecting to a data source, placing controls on the app screens, and finally publishing and sharing the app to make it accessible to consumers.

- The actual process of designing a canvas app involves placing controls on the app screens to create a usable interface for the consumers who will be running it.

- After developers finish building their apps, they have to save them and share them with the users who will access them.

- Model-driven apps are centered on the data they gather and present and the business processes they realize for users.

- Model-driven app designs are based on components, but in the classic App Designer interface, the components do not resemble the elements as they will appear on the final app screens. The newer, modern App Designer interface does provide a WYSIWYG experience.

- Forms appear in model-driven apps when users view data in a table format and click the New button to create a new record in the table.

Thought experiment

In this thought experiment, demonstrate your skills and knowledge of the topics covered in this chapter. You can find answers to this thought experiment in the next section.

Ralph is experimenting with Power Apps, the license for which he obtained with his Dynamics 365 subscription. He is trying to develop a canvas app that will allow his company's salespeople to enter order information on their smartphones. The orders are to be saved to an order entry database on the company's SQL Server. Ralph has created a suitable interface for the app, with fields in which the salespeople can specify the customers and the products they want to order. The app seems to be working properly during Ralph's in-house testing, but when he attempts a trial deployment to a small group of salespeople in the field, the order information is not being written to the SQL database. Which of the following could be the problem?

A. The salespeople are using a Power Apps version that does not support connections to a SQL Server.

B. The salespeople do not have adequate permissions to write to the SQL database.

C. The SQL Server is not accessible from a mobile data network.

Thought experiment answers

A, B, or C. Any of the three answers could potentially be the cause of the problem experienced by the salespeople.

    A.   If the salespeople are not using a Power Apps license that supports premium connectors (of which the SQL Server connector is one), they will not be able to access the database. Ralph has obtained his Power Apps license with his Dynamics 365 subscription, which includes support for premium connectors.

    B.   The salespeople must log on to the SQL Server to access the database, and if their accounts do not have the appropriate permissions, as Ralph's evidently does, they will not be able to save their order entry information to the database.

    C.   If the SQL Server is hosted by a physical computer in the company's data center, Ralph is presumably accessing it through the company network. The salespeople in the field might not be able to access the SQL Server using their mobile data networks from outside the company's facility.

CHAPTER 5

Demonstrate the capabilities of Power Automate

As the name implies, Microsoft Power Automate is a tool that allows developers to automate commonly performed repetitive tasks. Many applications have the ability to automate their own tasks, but Power Automate can automate sequences of tasks that involve multiple applications and services. For example, it is possible to use Power Automate to generate an email notification each time a tweet is posted that is addressed to a specific hashtag. The sequences of tasks Power Automate creates are called *flows*. In fact, the Power Automate product was until recently known as Microsoft Flow.

Skills covered in this chapter:

- Skill 5.1: Identify common Power Automate components
- Skill 5.2: Build a basic cloud flow

Skill 5.1: Identify common Power Automate components

Power Automate is a tool that does not require any coding knowledge; it uses a graphical interface in the Power Automate portal to create sequences of events called flows that are themselves divided into elements known as triggers and actions. A *trigger* is an event that launches the flow, and *actions* are the tasks that the flow performs after it is launched.

This skill covers how to:

- Identify flow types, including cloud, desktop, and business process flows
- Describe use cases for flows and available flow templates
- Describe how Power Automate uses connector triggers and actions
- Describe loops and conditions, including switch, do until, and apply to each
- Describe expressions
- Describe use cases for approvals
- Describe the Power Automate apps, including Power Automate Desktop, Power Automate mobile, and Power Automate portal

---

Identify flow types, including cloud, desktop, and business process flows

The Power Automate portal provides developers with dozens of flow templates. Flow templates are essentially combinations of various triggers and actions.

However, it is also possible to create a flow from scratch. When a user clicks the +New flow button on the My flows screen, a drop-down list appears, as shown in Figure 5-1, from which the user can opt to create a flow from a template or choose one of the following options:

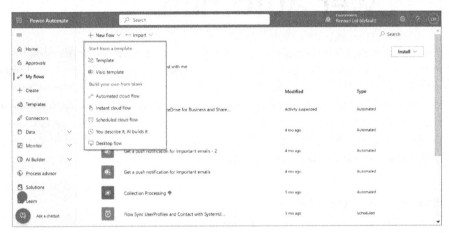

FIGURE 5-1 The New flow drop-down list on the My flows screen in the Power Automate portal

- *Automated cloud flow* (see Figure 5-2)—A flow that is triggered automatically when a specific event occurs, such as the arrival of an email or the posting of a file

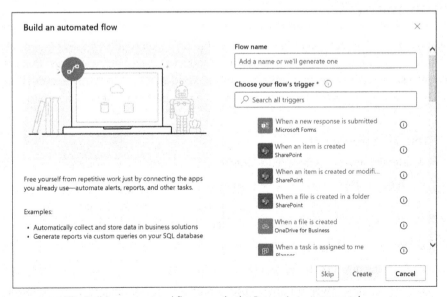

FIGURE 5-2 The Build an automated flow page in the Power Automate portal

- *Instant cloud flow* (see Figure 5-3)—A flow (also called a button flow) that is triggered manually by a user clicking or tapping a button or other control

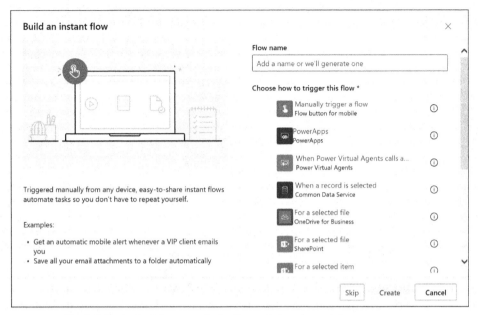

FIGURE 5-3 The Build an instant flow page in the Power Automate portal

- *Scheduled cloud flow* (see Figure 5-4)—A flow that is configured to launch at a specific date and time or by a recurring schedule

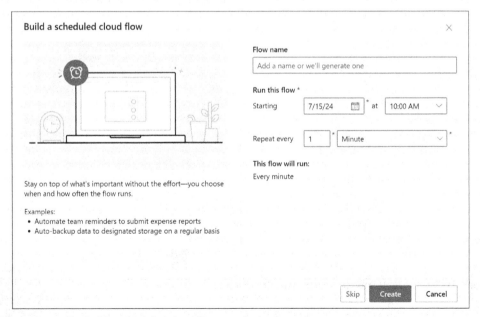

FIGURE 5-4 The Build a scheduled cloud flow page in the Power Automate portal

- *You describe it, AI builds it* (see Figure 5-5)—Enables users to create flows by describing them in plain language

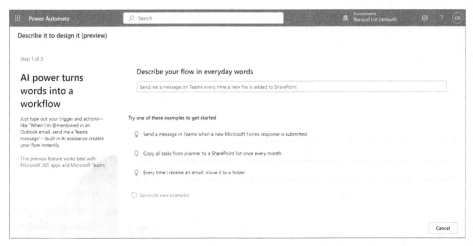

FIGURE 5-5 The Describe it to design it page in the Power Automate portal

- *Desktop flow* (see Figure 5-6)—Provides links to the Power Automate Desktop app, which creates flows that automate the playback of recorded tasks in legacy applications requiring mouse clicks and/or keyboard input

FIGURE 5-6 The Build a desktop flow page in the Power Automate portal

Describe use cases for flows and available flow templates

Power Platform has hundreds of connectors that provide access to Microsoft and third-party applications and services, which Power Automate developers can use in innumerable combinations when creating flows. The Power Automate tool can support advanced development projects, but it is actually designed for beginning users that Microsoft often calls *citizen developers*. To simplify the process of getting started in creating Power Automate flows, the tool also includes dozens of templates, a small sampling of which is shown in Figure 5-7.

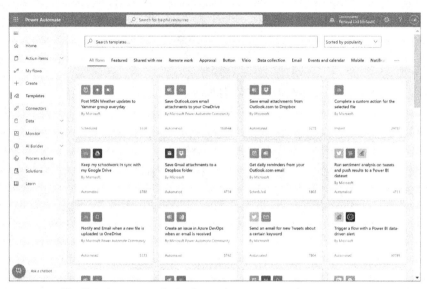

FIGURE 5-7 The Templates screen in the Power Automate portal

Templates are examples of flows using various combinations of connectors that are designed to perform common business tasks involving multiple applications and services. Each template appears as a tile, as shown in Figure 5-8, that contains a summary of the tasks the flow accomplishes, the template's author, how the flow is triggered, and icons indicating the connectors the flow will use.

FIGURE 5-8 The Notify me in Outlook when a student completes a quiz template tile in the Power Automate portal

For example, users can easily configure Microsoft Outlook to generate a notification in Windows 10 whenever a new email arrives; doing so does not require any special programming or outside software. However, if a teacher wants to receive Outlook email notifications whenever students submit quiz responses in Microsoft Forms, this requires communication between Forms and Outlook that is not readily possible within the applications themselves.

As shown in the previous figure, Power Automate includes a template for a flow that makes these notifications possible. When a user selects the template tile, a detail screen appears that summarizes the tasks performed by the flow and lists the connectors it will use, as shown in Figure 5-9.

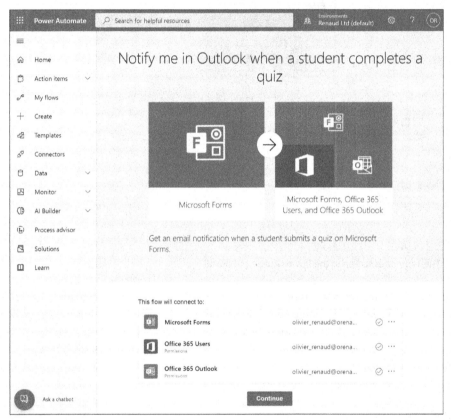

FIGURE 5-9 Detail screen for the Notify me in Outlook when a student completes a quiz flow template in the Power Automate portal

> **NOTE CONNECTOR CREDENTIALS**
>
> By default, most connectors will use the credentials of the currently logged-on user when accessing outside applications and services. If the given credentials do not authenticate properly, or if there is a reason to use a different account, the developer can switch accounts for a selected connector and supply new credentials.

Clicking Continue on the detail screen for the flow displays the workspace canvas containing the individual trigger and action elements of the flow, as shown in Figure 5-10. On this canvas, the developer provides the details needed for the flow to function. Controls are also available that the developer can use to customize the flow to perform additional tasks.

FIGURE 5-10 The workspace canvas for the Notify me in Outlook when a student completes a quiz template

A generic template like this one obviously cannot include all the details necessary for the flow to run. In this case, the developer must supply information such as the name of the form to monitor and the subject line and message text to be used in the notification emails.

Flows are not limited to one trigger and one action, and there are templates that perform multiple actions when triggered. For example, the template shown in Figure 5-11 expands on the previous one not only by sending a notification email, but also by storing the students' quiz responses in a SharePoint list.

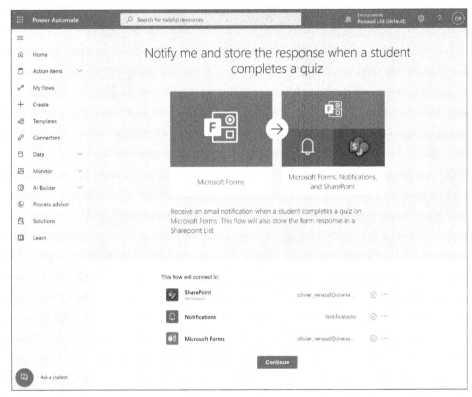

FIGURE 5-11 Detail screen for the Notify me and store the response when a student completes a quiz template in the Power Automate portal

The workspace canvas for this template, as shown in Figure 5-12, approaches the tasks somewhat differently than the previous one. This template uses the Notifications connector to send the email and adds a SharePoint action that saves the form response to a list selected by the developer.

FIGURE 5-12 The workspace canvas for the Notify me and store the response when a student completes a quiz template in the Power Automate portal

All the templates provided in the Power Automate portal can be used as is or modified to suit the needs of the developer. The bottom of the canvas always includes Add an action and New step buttons that open the Choose an operation dialog box, as shown in Figure 5-13, which the developer can use to add another task to the flow.

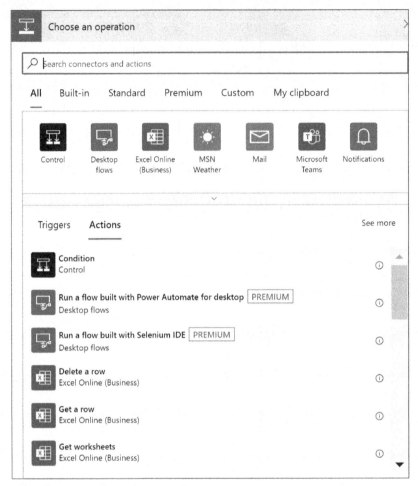

FIGURE 5-13 The Choose an operation dialog box from the workspace canvas for the Notify me and store the response when a student completes a quiz template in the Power Automate portal

The Templates screen in the Power Automate portal allows users to search for specific templates or browse through the tiles representing the hundreds of flow templates included with the tool. A series of tabs breaks the collection of templates down into categories, including the following:

- *All flows*—Displays all the available flow templates
- *Top picks*—Displays a selection of the most popular flow templates
- *Shared with me*—Displays flow templates that other users in the organization have shared with the current user
- *Remote work*—Displays a selection of flow templates appropriate for users working from remote locations
- *Approval*—Displays flow templates requesting or granting manager approval for specified tasks

- *Button*—Displays templates for instant flows that are triggered by a manual button click or tap
- *Visio*—Displays templates that allow developers to use Microsoft Visio to design workflows
- *Data collection*—Displays flow templates that save, copy, or move incoming data
- *Email*—Displays flow templates that manage or generate email messages
- *Calendar*—Displays flow templates that create and manage calendar events
- *Mobile*—Displays templates for flows that are designed for use on mobile clients
- *Notifications*—Displays flow templates that generate notifications
- *Productivity*—Displays flow templates that create and manage tasks in productivity applications, such as SharePoint and Teams
- *Social media*—Displays flow templates that perform tasks in social media applications
- *Sync*—Displays flow templates that copy, move, or synchronize files between accounts, folders, or applications

Describe how Power Automate uses connector triggers and actions

The Power Platform tools use connectors to access data sources in various ways. Power Automate uses connectors in flows for both triggers and actions.

> **NEED MORE REVIEW?** **CONNECTORS**
>
> For more information on connectors and their use in the Power Platform tools, see "Skill 2.2: Describe connectors" in Chapter 2, "Identify the core components of Microsoft Power Platform."

Connector types

Power Automate uses connectors to establish two basic types of data source connections:

- *Function-based*—Refers to connections that use functions to perform tasks on the source application or service. Triggers often use functions to monitor activity at the source, allowing them to launch a flow when a specific event occurs, such as the arrival of a file or email. Flows also use functions for actions, allowing them to send an email, create a calendar event, modify permissions, or generate a notification.
- *Tabular*—Refers to connections that allow a flow to retrieve data from the source application or service in a table format. Flows can use tabular data as triggers—to provoke an action when the data is changed, for example. However, flows more often use tabular data as part of an action—to copy it to another location, for example. When Power Apps uses a Power Automate flow as part of its functionality, it can conceivably use a connector to create, modify, or remove data on the source.

Connection permissions

When Power Automate uses a connector in a flow, it is nearly always necessary for the connector to authenticate to the outside application or service before it can access the data source. The connector must therefore have the credentials necessary to complete the authentication. When a flow uses multiple connections to different data sources, each connector must supply credentials to perform its own authentication.

When a developer creates a flow by selecting a template tile, a detail screen appears, the bottom half of which lists all the connectors needed for the flow, as shown in Figure 5-14, as well as the account names that will be used to establish the connections. Many connectors, by default, use the credentials of the currently logged-on user to connect to the data source, but this is not always appropriate or possible. The developer might want to use different accounts, or the user might prudently have different passwords for the various applications and services.

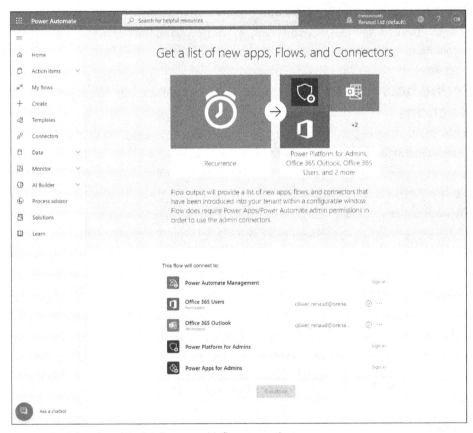

FIGURE 5-14 A flow template detail screen with five connections

In this particular template, the Office 365 Users and Office 365 Outlook connectors are using the current account, and the green check marks indicate that the connectors will authenticate successfully. The remaining three connectors have blue Sign in links, indicating that they are not prepared to authenticate and that the developer needs to specify the accounts they will use to access those data sources.

Until that is done, there is a grayed-out Continue button at the bottom of the screen; when all of the connectors are ready to authenticate, it changes to a blue Continue button, allowing the developer to move on in the process of creating the flow.

When the developer clicks one of the blue Sign in links or the Switch account button on a connector that already has an account listed, a Sign in to your account screen appears, as shown in Figure 5-15, in which the developer can select a user account or specify a new one. Depending on the connector and the nature of its authentication, the screen prompting for credentials might be different in appearance.

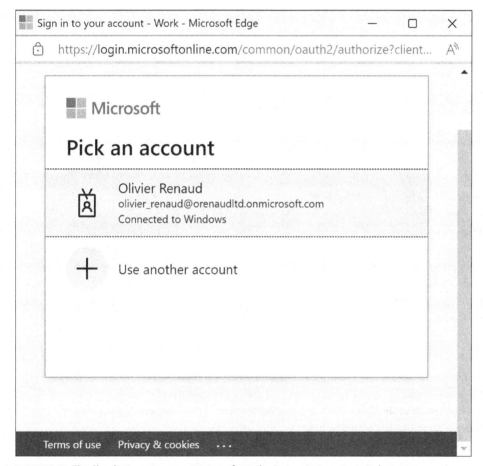

FIGURE 5-15 The Sign in to your account screen from the Power Automate portal

When a developer creates a flow from scratch or modifies an existing flow, it is always possible to change the credentials that a connector uses to authenticate with a data source. On the workspace canvas, every trigger and action step has a menu button on the right side.

The menu includes a My connections section, in which the developer can choose an existing account or click the +Add new connection button, as shown in Figure 5-16.

FIGURE 5-16 Two steps in a flow on the Power Automate workspace canvas

One important consideration for developers configuring connectors in Power Automate flows is whether they want the consumers of the flow to be able to use the same authentication credentials specified during its creation. When developers create automated flows, the credentials they specify for the connectors are used whenever the flow runs. Adding co-owners to an automated flow allows them to change the credentials as needed.

When developers create instant flows—flows that are manually triggered—they can designate other users as co-owners or run-only users. For run-only users, the developer can specify whether the consumers can use the credentials already supplied during the creation of the flow or must supply credentials of their own for the connectors. Consumers can then configure the flow to access their own accounts instead of the developer's, as in the case of a flow that must access the consumer's email.

EXAM TIP

Candidates for the PL-900 exam should be conscious of credential security issues when designing and building flows. There can be situations when a developer's use of administrative credentials while creating a flow can allow the flow's consumers to access sensitive data they should not be permitted to use.

Describe loops and conditions, including switch, do until, and apply to each

In its simplest form, a Power Automate flow consists of a series of steps performed in sequence, one trigger, and at least one action. When the last action is completed, the processing of the flow ends. However, it is possible to create more complex flows that take nonlinear paths, such as those that contain conditional branching or processing loops.

Conditional flows

A flow can contain a condition, which is an if/then statement that defines two possible actions. For example, an automated flow can contain a trigger that causes it to run whenever a new email arrives in a specific mailbox. A Condition action can then check whether the email message was sent with high importance, as shown in Figure 5-17. The Condition step then branches into two possible actions: the If yes action if the message was sent with high importance and the If no action if it was not. The If yes action can cause a notification to be sent to the user's smartphone, and the If no action does nothing.

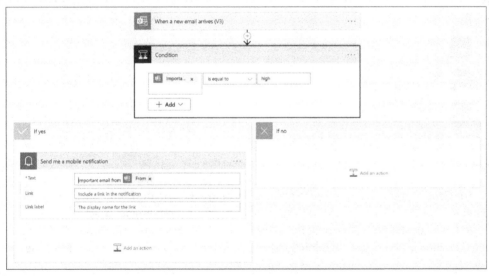

FIGURE 5-17 A Condition branch in an automated flow

To create a conditional branch, the developer creates a new step and, in the Choose an action dialog box, clicks the Built-in tab and selects the Condition action, as shown in Figure 5-18.

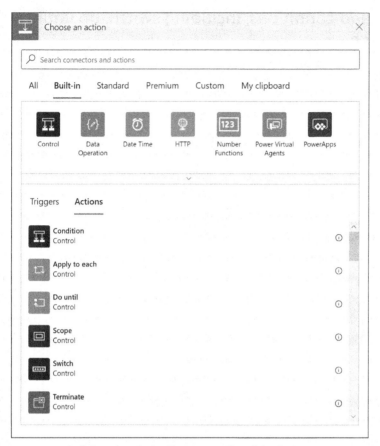

FIGURE 5-18 Built-in actions in the Choose an action dialog box

The Condition action is one way to create branching actions in the Power Automate flow; another is the Switch action, which is a conditional action that determines which of multiple cases to execute based on the input fed to the switch. The advantage of the Switch action over the Condition action is that although Condition is limited to two branches (Yes and No), the Switch action can have as many cases as are needed.

For example, the flow in Figure 5-19 contains an action that determines the day of the week, which is then followed by a Switch action that contains cases named for days of the week. Each case can then contain actions specific to that day. Clicking the plus sign to the right of Case 2 adds another case to the Switch.

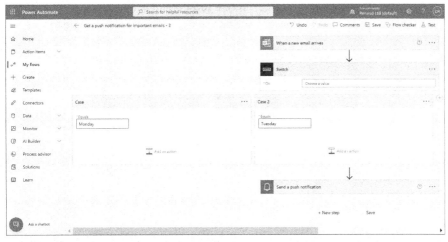

FIGURE 5-19 The Switch action with the first two cases

Looping flows

Looping refers to flows that contain sequences of actions that intentionally repeat. Two of the most common looping actions are Apply to each and Do until. Each of these actions performs a series of tasks repeatedly, until a particular condition causes the loop to end.

Apply to each is a loop action that retrieves an array of items (such as the 10 most recent emails received) and performs a subsequent action (or series of actions) on each of the items in the array. For example, the flow shown in Figure 5-20 first executes the Get emails (V3) action to retrieve the user's 10 most recent emails. Then, the Apply to each action executes the Condition action for the 10 emails, checking the value of the Importance field in each one. If an email is set to high importance, the Send me a mobile notification action executes; if not, then there is no further action. The looping action continues until all the items in the array have been processed.

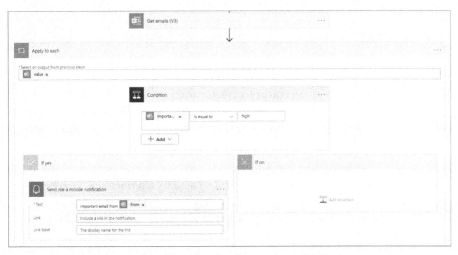

FIGURE 5-20 The Apply to each action with a Condition action inside the loop

Do until is a loop action that repeatedly performs a subsequent action (or series of actions) until a specified condition is met. For example, the flow in Figure 5-21 sets a variable to an integer value of 1. Then, the Do until action sets the loop to repeat until the variable reaches a value of 10. The Increment variable action within the Do until loop increases the variable by 1 each time it executes. The loop repeats until the value of the variable reaches 10.

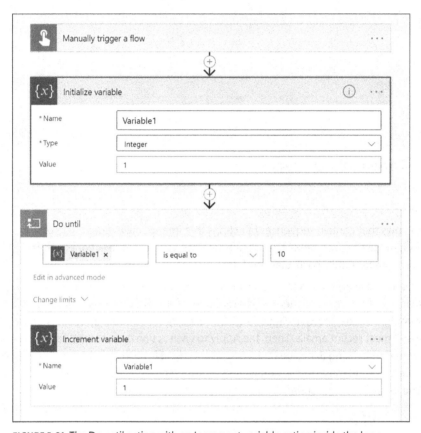

FIGURE 5-21 The Do until action with an Increment variable action inside the loop

Describe expressions

Power Automate provides a large collection of connectors with a wide selection of triggers and actions. Most of the triggers and actions have settings that the developer must configure before the flow will operate. Placing the mouse cursor in a text box causes a Dynamic content pop-up to appear.

This dialog box contains fields from the data source accessible by the connector. Selecting a field inserts a variable into the text box that is replaced by actual data when the flow executes. For example, selecting the Timestamp field inserts the Timestamp variable into the text box, as shown in Figure 5-22. When the flow runs, the variable will be replaced by the time stamp reflecting the date and time that the flow executed.

FIGURE 5-22 The Dynamic content pop-up dialog box with the Timestamp field selected

However, there are instances when developers might want to add operations that are not provided by an action's native settings. For these cases, Power Automate supports the use of expressions, which can perform operations on existing values.

The previous example uses the Get calendar view of events (V3) action and inserts the Timestamp variable into the Start Time text box. The action will therefore get the calendar events starting on the date and time the flow is executed. For the End Time value, the developer might want to get seven days' worth of calendar information. The field could accept an exact date and time, in the correct time stamp format, but this does not provide a permanent solution for the flow.

Instead, the developer can insert the addDays() expression, which can calculate an end time seven days from the date and time that the flow is executed. Selecting the Expression tab on the pop-up menu displays a list of expressions that can perform a variety of operations. The addDays() expression, as shown in Figure 5-23, takes as its parameters the time stamp from which the days will be added and the number of days to add (or subtract, using a negative value).

For the purpose of this example, the value for the End Time field will be as follows:

```
addDays (utcNow(),7)
```

The utcNow() expression returns the time stamp for the current date and time, so the addDays() expression will take the date and time when the flow executes and add seven days to it. Other date and time expressions allow developers to add hours, minutes, or seconds to a given time.

FIGURE 5-23 The Expression tab in the pop-up dialog box, with the addDays() expression selected

Expressions can perform many other functions apart from working with time stamps. The expressions that Power Automate uses are taken from the Workflow Definition Language in Azure Logic Apps and are organized into the following categories:

- *String functions*—Manipulate data strings by concatenating, replacing, splitting, trimming, formatting, and converting data

- *Collection functions*—Work with data arrays by specifying their length, locating empty strings, joining elements, and locating their first or last elements

- *Logical functions*—Perform comparisons using if/then statements, arithmetical functions, and Boolean operators

- *Conversion functions*—Convert input to different data types, such as integers, strings, Booleans, and XML or JSON values

- *Math functions*—Perform standard arithmetical functions, generate random values, and identify minimum and maximum values

- *Date and time*—Generate strings containing time stamps based on calendar functions, such as adding and subtracting time intervals and identifying the start of a time interval

- *Referencing functions*—Provide the ability to work with the inputs and outputs of other triggers and actions

- *Workflow functions*—Provide the ability to retrieve details about a flow and the URL of a trigger or action

- *URI parsing functions*—Retrieve specific information about URIs, including host names, queries, paths, ports, and schemes

- *Manipulation*—Retrieve information about and modify JSON and XML objects

NEED MORE REVIEW? EXPRESSIONS

For a schema reference guide to the Azure Logic Apps Workflow Definition Language that contains expressions usable in Power Automate, see https://docs.microsoft.com/en-us/azure/logic-apps/logic-apps-workflow-definition-language?.

Describe use cases for approvals

One of the common uses of Power Automate flows is to process approvals of documents in which users must seek the consent of a superior before the task they are working on is completed. For example, a file might require approval before it can be posted to a SharePoint site, or an email might require approval before a user can send it out to customers.

In many cases, an approval works by having users post documents to a temporary place, such as a SharePoint list. The temporary post triggers a flow, which contains an Approvals action. This action generates an approval request email and sends it to a designated user, as shown in Figure 5-24. An approval tile also appears on the user's Home page of the Power Automate portal. The user responds by approving or rejecting the document, and a Condition action takes appropriate action depending on the response.

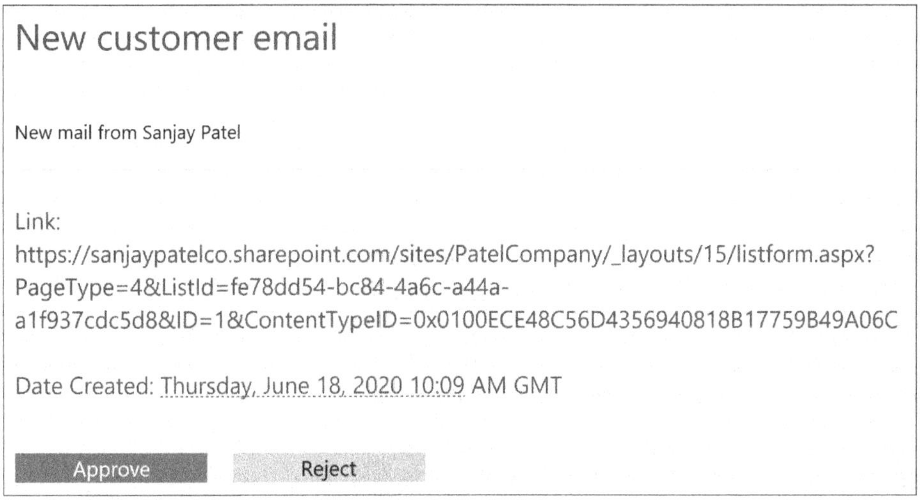
New customer email
New mail from Sanjay Patel
Link:
https://sanjaypatelco.sharepoint.com/sites/PatelCompany/_layouts/15/listform.aspx?PageType=4&ListId=fe78dd54-bc84-4a6c-a44a-a1f937cdc5d8&ID=1&ContentTypeID=0x0100ECE48C56D4356940818B17759B49A06C
Date Created: Thursday, June 18, 2020 10:09 AM GMT
Approve
Reject

FIGURE 5-24 An approval email generated by an Approvals action

In the example flow shown in Figure 5-25, users wanting to send an email to the organization's customers post the desired text in a SharePoint list called CustomerMail. This triggers the flow, which runs a Start an approval action, specifying the name of the person whose approval is sought and containing a link to the SharePoint item.

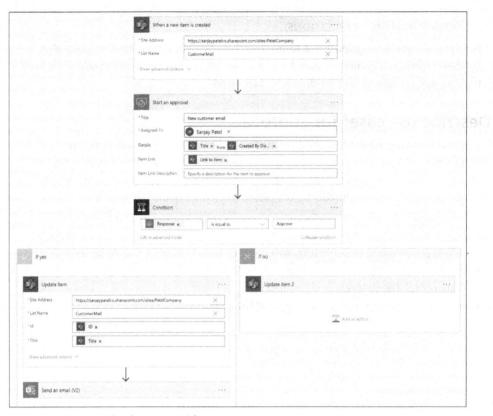

FIGURE 5-25 An example of an approval flow

When the approver's response is returned to the flow, the Start an approval action passes it down to a Condition action, which tests for a value of Yes in the Response field. In the If yes branch of the condition are actions that update the SharePoint item to register its approval and generate the email message for the customers. In the If no branch, there is just an Update item action that registers the No response in the SharePoint item.

Describe the Power Automate apps, including Power Automate Desktop, Power Automate mobile, and Power Automate portal

Microsoft Power Automate, in its original implementation, is a cloud-based service that users access through a web-based portal. The flows that users create are stored in the cloud, which makes them accessible to their data sources and to Power Apps. Power Automate and Power Apps are designed to work together; basing them both in the cloud—along with Microsoft Dataverse—makes that possible.

Power Automate mobile

In addition to the web portal, there are mobile versions of the Power Automate interface available for the Android, iOS, and Windows Phone platforms. These mobile apps provide an interface to the Power Automate cloud service, allowing both developers and consumers to access their apps for editing, testing, or execution.

Mobile users can display their flows, for example, as shown in Figure 5-26, as well as display their details and edit them. Consumers can run flows and, in the case of instant flows, launch them with a button push or other mechanism that the flow is configured to use as its trigger.

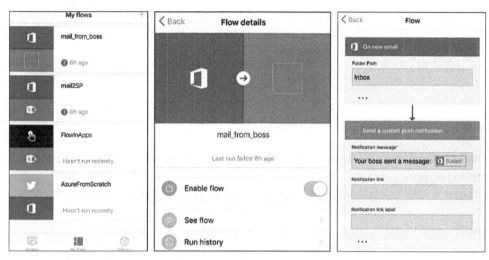

FIGURE 5-26 Screens from the Power Automate mobile app

Power Automate Desktop

There is also a desktop version of Power Automate, but unlike the mobile version, Power Automate Desktop is not just an interface to the cloud service. Desktop flows are different from the cloud flows that developers create in the Power Automate portal or the mobile app.

Desktop flows, as the name implies, are intended to automate repetitive desktop tasks. The Power Automate Desktop application has an interface that allows users to drag and drop actions onto a workspace, as shown in Figure 5-27. The desktop app can also record the user's keyboard and mouse actions and save them as flows, which they can run to repeat those actions at will.

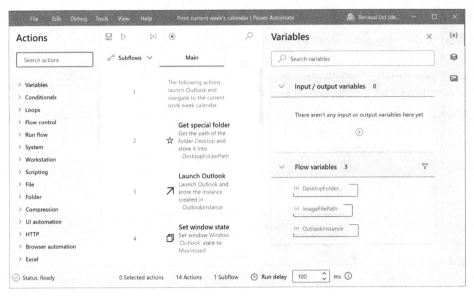

FIGURE 5-27 Power Automate Desktop workspace

As with cloud flows, desktop flows can automate interactions between unrelated applications and services, such as by manipulating files and folders, organizing incoming email messages, and saving data extracted from a website to a spreadsheet. Because they can capture actions at the user interface level, desktop flows can automate tasks performed by virtually any application, including terminal emulators and legacy apps.

Skill 5.2: Build a basic cloud flow

Power Automate provides three basic ways of creating a flow: one is to start from scratch by selecting a trigger type and adding actions from there, one is to choose from the many templates included with the tool, and the third is to start by choosing a connector and build from there.

This skill covers how to:

- Create a cloud flow by using the instant, automated, or scheduled flow template
- Modify a cloud flow
- Use flow steps to perform data operations
- Run a cloud flow

Create a cloud flow by using the instant, automated, or scheduled flow template

The Create page in the Power Automate portal, shown in Figure 5-28, provides several entries into the three flow creation methods, as follows:

- *Start from blank*—This section at the top of the screen contains tiles for the basic flow types. After selecting a trigger and creating the flow, you then populate it by adding actions.

- *Start from a template*—This section contains tiles for a small selection of the many templates available. There are several collections of templates directed toward specific business needs, such as those aimed at remote work, notifications, and approvals.

- *Start from a connector*—Below the templates (and not visible in the figure) is a section that contains tiles for a selection of the most commonly used connectors.

All of these are entries to the same basic process of creating and modifying a flow.

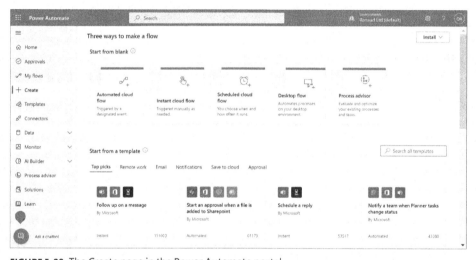

FIGURE 5-28 The Create page in the Power Automate portal

The first method is to start from a blank flow by selecting one of the tiles representing the type of trigger that will launch it. Selecting one of the tiles in the Start from blank section opens a screen containing configuration settings for the trigger, as shown in "Identify flow types, including cloud, desktop, and business process flows," earlier in this chapter. These screens function as follows:

- *Automated cloud flow*—To create an automated cloud flow, the developer must select a trigger that monitors some element of a connector for activity that launches the flow. For example, the trigger can launch the flow in response to the arrival of a message or the creation of a document in an application or service.

- *Instant* (also called button) *cloud flow*—To create an instant (or button) cloud flow, the developer must select a trigger that responds to an action by the flow user. The trigger can be linked to a button pressed in the Power Automate mobile app or an activity in another application or service, such as selecting a file or other object.

- *Scheduled cloud flow*—To create a scheduled cloud flow, the developer must specify a date and time for the flow to launch and, if necessary, a repeat interval.

- *Desktop flow*—To create desktop flows, the developer must open or download the Power Automate Desktop app.

EXAM TIP

Candidates for the PL-900 exam should be conscious of the fact that the instant flow type currently referenced in the exam objective was at one time called the button flow type. Some sources might still use the old nomenclature.

In the case of the automated, instant, and scheduled flows, the opening screen specifies how and when the flow will launch.

Using the Power Automate workspace canvas

After the developer has configured the trigger for an automated, instant, or scheduled flow in the Power Automate portal, the workspace canvas for the flow appears, as shown in Figure 5-29. In this example, an automated flow is triggered each time a new email arrives at the user's Outlook 365 Inbox. By default, the trigger uses the account of the user that is currently logged on, although it is possible to create a new connection to a different email address, if desired.

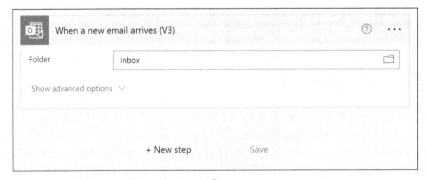

FIGURE 5-29 A trigger in a Power Automate flow

With the trigger in place, the developer can then click the New step button to open the Choose an action dialog box, as shown in Figure 5-30. Power Automate provides hundreds of actions that developers can use to manage the incoming email messages. For example, Control actions can evaluate the email messages and take action on what they find. Notification actions can inform the user when certain types of emails arrive. This example will use both of these action types.

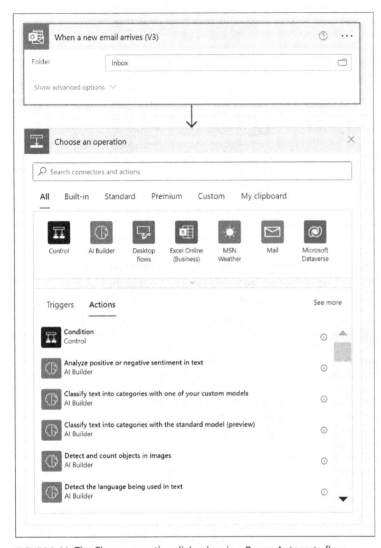

FIGURE 5-30 The Choose an action dialog box in a Power Automate flow

Selecting the Condition action adds three boxes to the workspace canvas, as shown in Figure 5-31: the Condition box and, branching from that, an If yes and an If no box.

FIGURE 5-31 A Condition action in a Power Automate flow

In the Condition box, the developer creates an if/then statement that can examine some part of the incoming email. Clicking in the Choose a value text box opens the Dynamic content pop-up, as shown in Figure 5-32, which lists the various fields in an email.

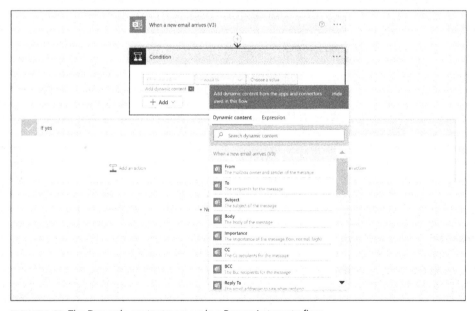

FIGURE 5-32 The Dynamic content pop-up in a Power Automate flow

The Condition box can test the value of any field in the email and return a Yes or No response. For example, after selecting the Importance field, the developer can type one of the acceptable values for that field in the Choose a value box. In this example, the condition being tested is whether Importance is equal to high, as shown in Figure 5-33. In the same way, the developer could use the Condition box to test whether the From field contains the name of a specific person or the Subject field contains a specific text string.

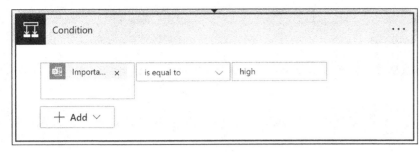

FIGURE 5-33 A Condition equation in a Power Automate flow

The If yes and If no boxes take action based on the results of the equation in the Condition box. If an email is set to have high importance, the Condition result is yes, and the flow executes any actions in the If yes box.

Clicking Add an action in the If yes box opens the same Choose an action dialog box shown earlier. In this example, high-importance emails cause the flow to execute the Send me a mobile notification action, as shown in Figure 5-34. The developer can type any message in the Text box and include values from fields selected in the Dynamic content pop-up. In this case, the notification will specify the sender of the email.

FIGURE 5-34 A Send me a mobile notification action in the If yes box in a Power Automate flow

The developer can create additional actions in the If yes box, if desired, such as an action that stores the email in a SharePoint site or copies any attachments to the user's OneDrive. The If no box can contain actions also, or be left blank, as needed.

Once the flow is complete, the developer should click Save to make sure that the flow is added to the user's My flows list, as shown in Figure 5-35.

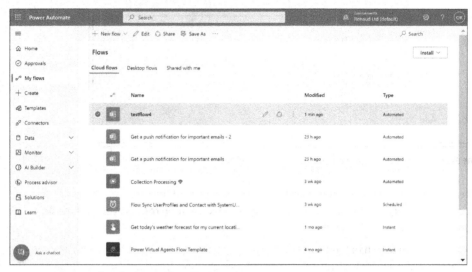

FIGURE 5-35 A new flow in the My flows list in Power Automate

Modify a cloud flow

For many new developers, the easiest way to learn how to build a flow is to begin with one of the flow templates included with Power Automate. A template includes the trigger and all of the actions needed to complete the flow's designated tasks, although some configuration of the elements might be needed to render the flow fully operational.

Many of the Power Automate flow templates are designed to transfer data from one application or service to another. For example, the Copy files between OneDrive for Business and SharePoint template, shown in Figure 5-36, creates an automated flow that monitors a specified OneDrive folder and copies all the files saved there to a specific SharePoint folder. The flow also checks for the success of the copy operation and generates an email if it fails.

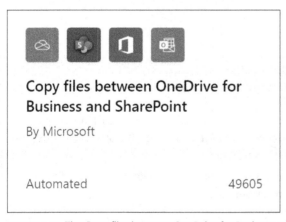

FIGURE 5-36 The Copy files between OneDrive for Business and SharePoint flow template tile

A template such as this one needs some modification before it can run. The developer must specify which OneDrive folder the trigger should monitor and choose the SharePoint site and the folder on it where the incoming files will be stored. The template detail screen, shown in Figure 5-37, includes drop-down lists in which the developer can configure the necessary fields.

FIGURE 5-37 The Copy files between OneDrive for Business and SharePoint flow template detail screen

The template also provides a list of the connectors the flow will use, which the developer can modify to use different credentials as needed. The flow then appears in the Power Automate workspace canvas, as shown in Figure 5-38.

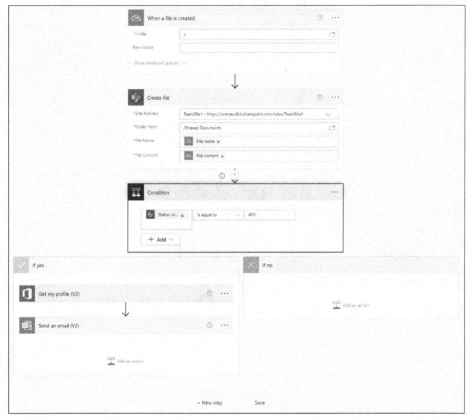

FIGURE 5-38 The workspace canvas for the Copy files between OneDrive for Business and SharePoint flow template

In this template, the flow's trigger monitors the specified OneDrive folder and, when files appear in it, the SharePoint Create file action uses the OneDrive File Name and File Content values to copy the files to the specified SharePoint folder. Then, a Condition action checks the status code of the SharePoint file creation and, if the value is 403 (Forbidden), the If yes branch generates an email to the user indicating that the task has failed.

Once the workspace canvas appears with the specified OneDrive and SharePoint folders, the work of the template is complete. The trigger and actions shown on the canvas are no different than if the developer created the flow from scratch. This means that it is possible for the developer to modify the flow as needed by changing the existing actions, inserting new actions, or altering the order in which the actions are executed.

Modifying actions

Whether a trigger or action is created by a template or added manually, a developer can always modify their configuration. By default, triggers and actions use the currently logged-on user's account to establish a connection to an application or service. Clicking the menu button in the trigger or action displays a context menu with a My connections section, as shown in Figure 5-39, in which the developer can select a different user account or add a new connection.

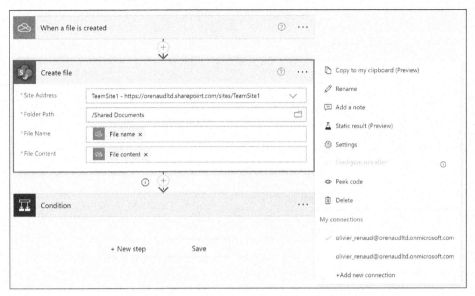

FIGURE 5-39 The context menu for a SharePoint Create file action

When the developer changes the connection to use a different account, the drop-down lists and the Dynamic content fields for the action change as well. In this example, the Site Address and Folder Path fields have drop-down lists that provide access to the current user's SharePoint environment. Changing the user address for the connection changes the contents of the drop-down lists. The File Name and File Content values are dynamic content fields that reference the OneDrive connection established in the trigger, so changing the connection in the trigger above changes the fields available in the Dynamic content pop-up.

Inserting actions

Developers can add actions to a flow in multiple ways. The Power Automate workspace canvas always includes a +New step button at the bottom, which opens the Choose an action dialog box. Selecting an action from the dialog box adds it to the bottom of the flow. The arrows pointing down from the trigger to the first action and from one action to another display a plus sign when the cursor hovers over them, allowing a developer to insert an action between two existing steps. Clicking the plus sign displays a menu with two options:

- *Add an action*—Opens the Choose an action dialog box, in which the developer can select an action to be inserted between the existing steps.
- *Add a parallel branch*—Opens the Choose an action dialog box in a separate branch off of the step above, as shown in Figure 5-40. This allows the flow to perform two separate actions at the same time, both using the results of the same previous step.

FIGURE 5-40 Two actions in a parallel branch off of a single trigger

Use flow steps to perform data operations

When working with data from various sources, it is sometimes necessary to modify the data format to make the sources compatible. Power Automate's Data Operation actions make it possible to reuse and reformat the data from previous actions in various ways:

- *Compose*—Allows the developer to type a data string into the Inputs field, as shown in Figure 5-41, and reuse that string later. In a subsequent action, the developer can select the Outputs field from the Compose section in the Dynamic content pop-up to insert the string from the Inputs field in the Compose action.

FIGURE 5-41 The Compose action in the Power Automate workspace canvas

- *Create CSV table*—Allows the developer to convert a data array into a table in CSV (comma-separated values) format, as shown in Figure 5-42. In this example, the array of usernames taken from the body of the previous action will be reformatted into the following table:

```
FirstName,LastName
Sanjay,Patel
Joanna,Yuan
```

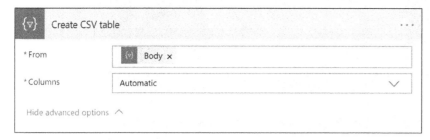

FIGURE 5-42 The Create CSV table action in the Power Automate workspace canvas

- *Create HTML table*—Allows the developer to convert a data array into an HTML (Hypertext Markup Language) table.
- *Filter array*—Allows the developer to apply a filter to a data array using an equation to select specific entries, as shown in Figure 5-43. In this example, an array consisting of usernames will be filtered to include only those users with a last name of Patel.

FIGURE 5-43 The Filter array action in the Power Automate workspace canvas

- *Join*—Allows the developer to modify a data array to use a different delimiter, as shown in Figure 5-44. In this example, the array of addresses in the From field is delimited by commas. Specifying a semicolon in the Join with field ensures that the resulting output will be the same array but delimited with semicolons.

FIGURE 5-44 The Join action in the Power Automate workspace canvas

- *Parse JSON*—Allows the developer to interpret the JSON output from a previous action by specifying a sample schema, as shown in Figure 5-45. The developer can then use the Dynamic content pop-up for a following action to select specific Parse JSON fields derived from the sample schema.

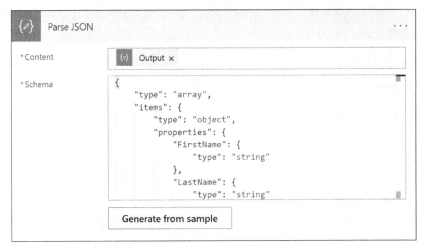

FIGURE 5-45 The Parse JSON action in the Power Automate workspace canvas

- *Select*—Allows the developer to reshape a data array to suit a different application or service, as shown in Figure 5-46. In this example, an array of names using the labels first and last, such as [{ "first": "Sanjay", "last": "Patel" }, { "first": "Joanna", "last": "Yuan" }], will be remapped to use the labels FirstName and LastName instead, as in [{ "FirstName": "Sanjay", "LastName": "Patel" }, { "FirstName": "Joanna", "LastName": "Yuan" }].

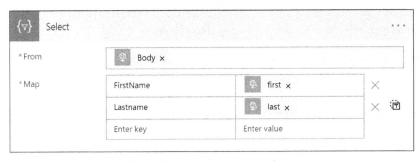

FIGURE 5-46 The Select action in the Power Automate workspace canvas

Run a cloud flow

After the developer has finished building a flow and has saved it so that it appears in the My flows list, it is ready to run, based on the type of trigger it uses. An automated flow will run when the event specified in the trigger occurs. An instant flow will run when a user deliberately triggers it by tapping a button or selecting an item. A scheduled flow will run when the specified date and time arrive.

To test a flow and examine how each step executes, the developer can click the Test button at the upper right of the workspace canvas. This opens a Test Flow pane, which provides options for starting the flow by performing the trigger action manually, using the data from previous runs, as shown in Figure 5-47, or using data selected from the trigger application, in this case OneDrive for Business.

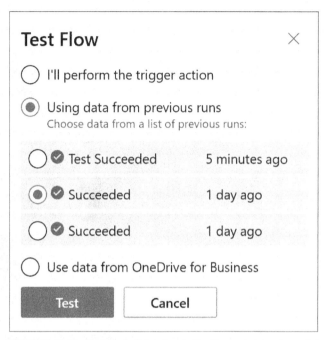

FIGURE 5-47 The Test Flow dialog box in the Power Automate portal

After the test run begins, the developer can monitor the performance of each step on the screen. Successfully executed steps have a circled check mark and failed steps have an X. Expanding each completed step in the flow displays detailed input and output information for that step, as shown in Figure 5-48.

For a step that has failed, an error message appears describing the reason for the failure, as shown in Figure 5-49. In this example, the Condition action exists only to send an email to the user in the event that the SharePoint Create file action fails. The Create file action was successful in this case, so despite the Condition action having failed, the overall execution of the flow is shown as having succeeded.

value
[
    {
        "id": "AAMkADg2ZWI0ZjNjLWFiMTYtNDQ0OC1hMzgzLTIwNWN1NmRhZTMwMgBG
        "receivedDateTime": "2020-06-21T08:44:51+00:00",
        "hasAttachments": false,
        "internetMessageId": "<faabcc1d1f0a4b749f5705b1ea40a9c1-JFBVALK
        "subject": "Renew your Microsoft subscriptions",

FIGURE 5-48 Flow test run results

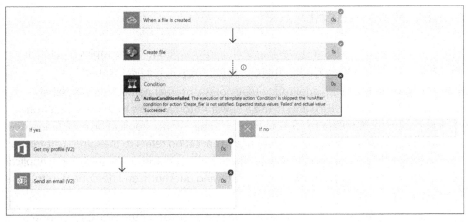

FIGURE 5-49 Flow test run results with a failed action

Chapter summary

- Power Automate supports five flow types: automated, instant, scheduled, desktop, and business process.
- To simplify the process of getting started in creating Power Automate flows, the tool also includes dozens of templates.
- Power Automate uses connectors to access data sources in flows for both triggers and actions.
- A flow can contain a condition, which is an if/then statement that defines two possible actions. *Looping* refers to flows that contain sequences of actions that intentionally repeat.
- Power Automate supports the use of expressions, which can perform operations on existing values.
- One of the common uses of Power Automate flows is to process approvals of documents, in which users must seek the approval of a superior before the task they are working on is completed.
- One method of creating a flow is to start from a blank flow by selecting one of the tiles in the Power Automate portal representing the type of trigger that will launch it.
- For many new developers, the easiest way to learn how to build a flow is to begin with one of the flow templates included with Power Automate. Templates often need some modification before they can run.
- Power Automate's Data Operation actions make it possible to reuse and reformat the data from previous actions in various ways.
- To test a flow and examine how each step executes, the developer can click the Test button at the upper right of the workspace canvas.

Thought experiment

In this thought experiment, demonstrate your skills and knowledge of the topics covered in this chapter. You can find the answers to this thought experiment in the next section.

Ralph is working with a British application that stores customer names using the labels Christian Name and Surname. He wants to use a Power Automate flow to transfer data from the British application's database to an American customer service application each time a new customer record is created. However, the American application refers to the same customer name data fields as First Name and Last Name. There are connectors available for both applications. Based on this information, respond to the following questions, and describe the structure of the required flow.

1. How can Ralph reconcile the differently named data fields for the two applications?

2. How can Ralph transfer the customer names obtained from one application to the other?

Thought experiment answers

This section contains the solution to the thought experiment. Each answer explains why the answer choice is correct.

1. The flow should use the connector for the British application as the trigger, launching the flow each time a new customer record is created. After the trigger, add a Select action with the output from the trigger placed in the From field and Map values that equate the labels: Christian Name with First Name and Surname with Last Name.

2. After reconciling the data field names, Ralph should add an action for the American application using the output from the Select action as input.

CHAPTER 6

Demonstrate the capabilities of Power Virtual Agents

Power Virtual Agents is the most recent addition to the Power Platform toolkit; it allows developers to create chatbots that provide customer service functionality without having to write code. A *chatbot* is a pop-up window that appears on a user's screen and provides a realistic dialogue experience with the consumer, furnishing genuine responses to customer service queries and even taking action at the customer's request.

Skills covered in this chapter:

- Skill 6.1: Describe the capabilities of Power Virtual Agents in Microsoft Teams
- Skill 6.2: Build and publish a basic chatbot

Skill 6.1: Describe the capabilities of Power Virtual Agents in Microsoft Teams

Chatbots have long been seen as a useful and economical means of providing customer service, but the development process involved in creating them was often lengthy and troublesome. This was, in large part, because of the constant communication required between the development and customer service departments, both prior to and subsequent to the deployment of the bot. The customer service people know what the bot has to do, and the development people know how to write the code to make the bot do it. Power Virtual Agents, by virtue of its no-code or low-code development requirements, allows the customer service personnel themselves to create chatbots and update them as needed when circumstances change.

This skill covers how to:
- Describe use cases for Power Virtual Agents within Microsoft Teams
- Describe topics, entities, and actions
- Describe message nodes, question nodes, conditions, trigger phrases, and the authoring canvas

---

Describe use cases for Power Virtual Agents within Microsoft Teams

Customer service and first-tier technical support services are always expensive propositions. This cost can be particularly galling for organizations when most customer issues are so simple and repetitive that it does not seem worth paying live representatives to give the same answers over and over. Live support can also be frustrating to customers when they discover that the hours they can interact with a live person are limited or that they must wait in a queue for the next available representative.

Chatbots were created to take over these repetitive and time-consuming tasks from live telephone and chat personnel. A bot with a script designed to provide basic information to customers can answer the simple questions at any time of the day or night, leaving the more complicated issues to the live representatives.

Citizen developers

As time has passed and the value of chatbots has been recognized by more organizations, the bots have been enhanced to take on more complex tasks themselves, even using artificial intelligence (AI) to perform actions instead of just supplying information. One of the main problems with these increasingly complex chatbots is that they require an extensive development effort.

In a chatbot development project, a gap has always existed between the people who know what tasks the bot has to perform and those who know how to make the bot do them. This gap is particularly problematic for organizations in which the customer service and technical support requirements change frequently. One of the primary design objectives for Power Virtual Agents, as with the other Power Platform tools, is to reduce that gap by making it possible for the customer service and technical support people to function as *citizen developers* by creating and updating the chatbots themselves.

Power Virtual Agents provides a guided graphical development environment that allows these citizen developers to create chatbots by specifying the questions most commonly asked by customers and then supplying possible answers to the questions. This strategy allows the bot to lead the customers through a branching dialogue, such as that shown in Figure 6-1, which leads them to a satisfactory answer to their question.

The Power Virtual Agents development interface allows the personnel familiar with customers' questions to program the bot with appropriate responses that they themselves would otherwise supply. More important, when the questions change or new questions arise, these same people can modify the bot to accommodate the organization's changing needs. In other environments, updating a bot can require a lengthy period of latency as the software goes back to a developer for changes to the code, retesting, and redeployment.

FIGURE 6-1 A branching dialogue in a Power Virtual Agents chatbot

Artificial intelligence

The ultimate goal of any chatbot is to make the customers believe that they are conversing with a real person. That might or might not be possible, depending on the effort put into the bot's development and on the sophistication of the customer, but Power Virtual Agents includes AI capabilities that allow it to engage the customer in realistic exchanges.

For example, the phrases that the developer supplies—the phrases that the customer can use in the conversation with the bot—might include "help me," "I need help," and many others. However, there are any number of other variations that a customer might also use, which the developer could not possibly anticipate. By supplying Power Virtual Agents with a selection of common phrases, it uses a form of AI called natural language understanding (NLU) to extrapolate others and accommodate many of the alternatives that customers might supply.

Taking action

Because it is part of the Power Platform toolkit, Power Virtual Agents can also work in conjunction with the other tools. The same connectors that allow Power Apps and Power Automate to interact with outside applications and services are available to Power Virtual Agents as well. This allows chatbots to not just dispense prerecorded information, but also to perform actions in response to customer requests by calling flows or apps and connecting to external data sources.

EXAM TIP

Candidates for the PL-900 exam should be conscious of the warnings that Microsoft includes with the Power Virtual Agents documentation, specifying that the product is not intended for use in emergency situations or for diagnosing or treating medical conditions, and that Microsoft abjures all responsibility for situations arising from the use of chatbots created by Power Virtual Agents subscribers.

Publishing chatbots

Publishing a chatbot makes it available to consumers. Whenever developers make changes to chatbots, they must republish them for consumers to see those changes. When a developer publishes a chatbot for the first time, Power Virtual Agents makes it available for testing on a demo website, as shown in Figure 6-2.

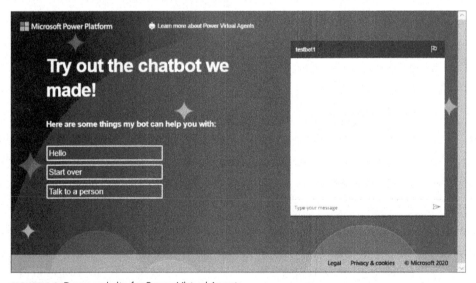

FIGURE 6-2 Demo website for Power Virtual Agents

Arguably, the place where consumers are most likely to encounter chatbots is on websites, but developers can publish their chatbots to many types of platforms other than websites, including internal messaging platforms, such as Microsoft Teams; mobile apps; and social media. Power Virtual Agents refers to these places of publication as *channels*, some of which are shown in the Power Virtual Agents portal, as shown in Figure 6-3.

FIGURE 6-3 The Channels page in the Power Virtual Agents portal

NEED MORE REVIEW? **CHANNELS**

For a complete list of the channels supported by Power Virtual Agents, expand the Manage menu item in the navigation pane of the Power Virtual Agents portal and select Channels.

Developers can publish a single chatbot to more than one channel. When a developer publishes a chatbot to multiple channels, modifying the bot and republishing it causes it to be refreshed on all the channels in which it appears.

Describe topics, entities, and actions

A chatbot has to understand what the user is saying and react appropriately, even when the user says something unexpected. Power Virtual Agents uses elements such as topics, entities, and actions to do this.

Topics

Power Virtual Agents simplifies the process of creating and configuring a chatbot by breaking the conversation between the bot and the user down into discrete elements called *topics*. For example, the first topic for a chatbot might be a greeting that welcomes the user and introduces the bot's purpose. The Topics page in the Power Virtual Agents portal, shown in Figure 6-4, contains a selection of basic system topics and also allows the developer to create new ones from scratch.

FIGURE 6-4 The Topics page in the Power Virtual Agents portal

As noted earlier, a topic begins with a trigger phrase, which is a list of possible phrases that the user might supply, which the bot understands and uses to initiate a particular conversation topic. The greeting topic, for example, might include "Hi," "Hello," and "Good morning" in its list of trigger phrases.

A conversation will typically span multiple topics, with the bot configured to launch a specific new topic based on the user's responses to the bot's questions. For example, at the end of the greeting topic, the developer might have the bot ask the user to specify the product with which they are experiencing a problem. When the user responds with a product name, as shown in Figure 6-5, the developer can select Go to another topic and link to a topic specific to that product.

FIGURE 6-5 Linking topics

Entities

In Power Virtual Agents, the term *entity* has a different meaning than it ever had in the Common Data Service. Now, in the Microsoft Dataverse, entities are known as tables. However, the term is still used in Power Virtual Agents, where an entity is essentially a dictionary of terms and phrases that a bot's artificial intelligence uses to identify a concept in a conversation. This aids the bot in understanding what the user is saying, even when the language the user employs is not an exact match to one of the trigger phrases in the topic's list.

The Entities page in the Power Virtual Agents portal, shown in Figure 6-6, contains a list of prebuilt entities that help bots to understand many common conversational concepts. These entities provide examples of syntax for these concepts that help the bot to understand what the user is saying.

FIGURE 6-6 The Entities page in the Power Virtual Agents portal

For example, there are many ways that users can reference specific dates or times in conversation. The user might refer to "last Thursday," or "December 25," or "3pm," all of which are easily comprehensible to another person but are not understandable to a bot unless it has some frame of reference for those expressions. The Date and time entity, shown in Figure 6-7, contains examples of these expressions and provides translations into saved values, which are time stamps that the bot can understand.

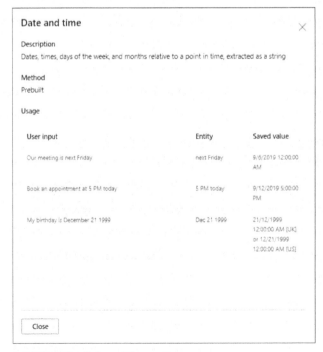

FIGURE 6-7 The Date and time entity

The prebuilt entities included with Power Virtual Agents provide bots with standard business terminology, but some organizations require bots to handle conversations involving specialized vocabulary. To accommodate these needs, developers can create custom closed lists or regular expression entities using the interface shown in Figure 6-8, in which they can specify terms and synonyms by which users might refer to them.

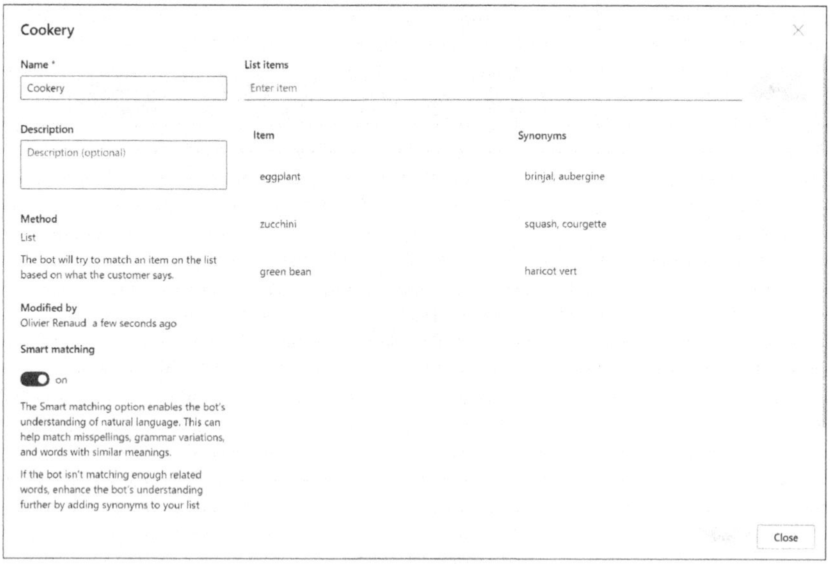

FIGURE 6-8 The entity creation interface

To use an entity when configuring a bot to ask a question, a developer selects the appropriate entity in the Identify selector, as shown in Figure 6-9.

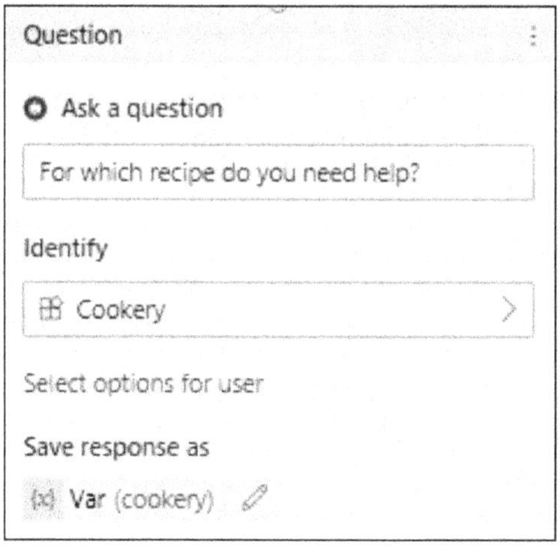

FIGURE 6-9 Using an entity in a bot

Actions

An *action*, as the word implies, is an element that allows a Power Virtual Agents bot to actually do something beyond conversing with the user. When a developer creates a new node in the Power Virtual Agents workspace, as shown in Figure 6-10, selecting Call an action provides various options, including the ability to authenticate the user with an identity provider, such as Azure Active Directory, or create a flow using Power Automate.

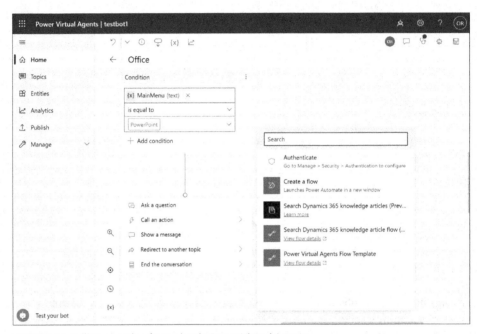

FIGURE 6-10 Calling an action from a bot in Power Virtual Agents

A bot can call an existing flow as long as it exists in the same environment as the bot, or the developer can create a new flow from scratch. By working in tandem with Power Automate, a Power Virtual Agents chatbot can perform a wide variety of tasks to service the user, including retrieving information from a database or service.

> **NOTE** **BOT AND FLOW INTERACTION**
> Power Automate flows can interact with Power Virtual Agents bots by exchanging data. To relay information to and from a data source using a flow, Power Virtual Agents creates variables that the developer can then use elsewhere in the topic.

Describe message nodes, question nodes, conditions, trigger phrases, and the authoring canvas

The creation and configuration of chatbots takes place on the *authoring canvas* in the Power Virtual Agents portal, as shown in Figure 6-11. The canvas is similar in appearance to that of Power Automate, with elements called nodes connected by flow lines. The nodes in a chatbot are processed vertically, from top to bottom, with some nodes branching into multiple streams that can take the conversation with the user to different topics.

FIGURE 6-11 The Power Virtual Agents authoring canvas

A chatbot conversation begins with a topic containing *trigger phrases*, which are the terms that the bot will recognize and to which it will respond. As noted earlier, the bot is capable of using AI to extrapolate additional phrases based on the trigger phrases supplied by the developer. When creating a topic, Power Virtual Agents calls for at least 5 to 10 trigger phrases. However, the Greeting system topic provided contains dozens of phrases synonymous with "Hello," as shown in Figure 6-12.

Trigger phrases (52)   ✕

Trigger phrases teach the bot different ways someone might ask about this topic. Natural language understanding helps identify a topic based on meaning and not exact words. To start learning, the bot needs 5-10 short trigger phrases. Learn more

Show writing tips

Add phrases

Enter text   +

To add phrases in bulk, paste in line-separated phrases or use Shift+Enter to create line separation

Good afternoon

Good morning

Hello

Hello agent!

Hello and good morning to you

Hello can you help me?

Hello can you please help me

Hello friend

Hello good afternoon

Hello good evening

Hello greeting

Hello how are you

Hello how are you doing?

FIGURE 6-12 Trigger phrases in the Greeting topic

Developers can add nodes anywhere in the bot by clicking the Add node plus sign button beneath an existing node or between two nodes. This opens a menu like the one shown in Figure 6-13, which enables the developer to add a node that does one of the following:

- Asks a question
- Calls an action
- Shows a message
- Redirects the conversation to another topic
- Ends the conversation

FIGURE 6-13 Adding a node in the Power Virtual Agents authoring canvas

Adding a *message node* displays a simple text box, as shown in Figure 6-14, in which the developer can type a message that will appear to the bot user.

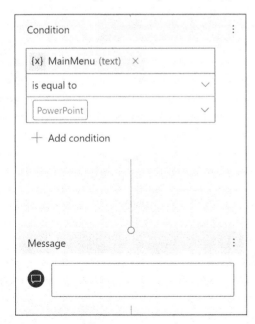

FIGURE 6-14 Adding a message node

Adding a *question node* inserts a dialog box in which the developer can type the text of a question and also specify the nature of the answer that the user will supply, as shown in Figure 6-15.

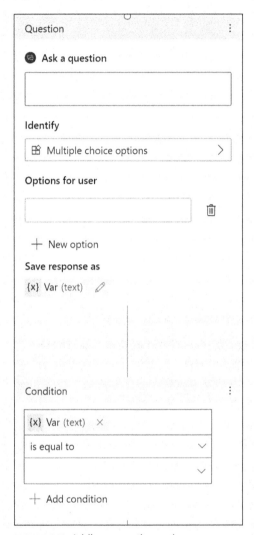

FIGURE 6-15 Adding a question node

The Identify drop-down list, shown in Figure 6-16, enables the developer to specify the type of information that the user will supply in response to the question. Selecting Multiple choice options, for example, enables the developer to supply possible answers to the question, from which the users can choose. The Identify list also includes entities that specify the type of data that the response to the question will contain, such as names, locations, dates, and times.

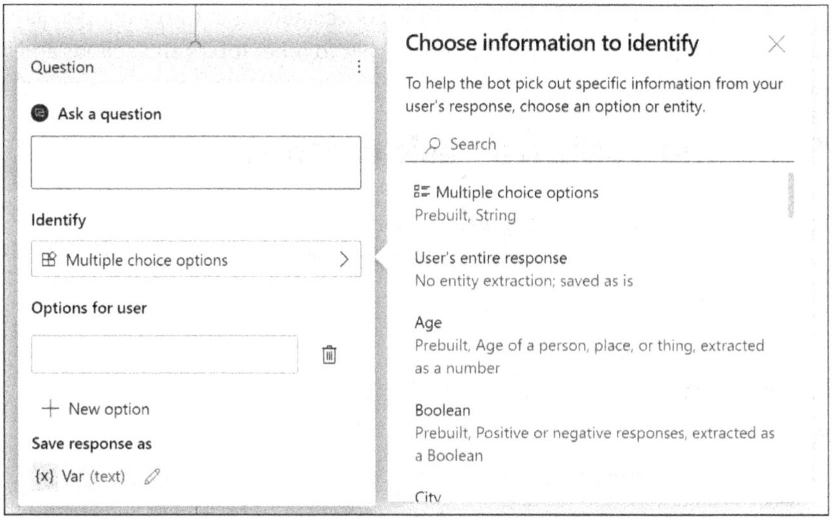

FIGURE 6-16 Choosing information to identify in a question node

The Options for user text box is where the developer supplies the possible answers to the question. Clicking the +New option button makes it possible to add as many possible answers as necessary. The dialog box also specifies the name of a variable that will contain the user's response to the question.

When a developer configures a question node with answers for the user to choose from, Virtual Power Agents creates a *condition node* for each possible answer and branches them off of the question node, as shown in Figure 6-17.

FIGURE 6-17 Condition nodes generated by a question node

Each of the condition nodes forms a new branch of the conversation that the developer can extend with additional questions and messages, as well as calls to other topics and actions and even to Power Automate flows.

Skill 6.2: Build and publish a basic chatbot

Power Virtual Agents simplifies the process of creating chatbots by eliminating the need to write code and providing a graphical design interface. The following sections examine the steps involved in creating and running a chatbot.

> **This skill covers how to:**
> - Create a chatbot
> - Create a topic
> - Call an action
> - Launch a Power Automate flow from a chatbot
> - Publish a chatbot

Create a chatbot

After starting Power Virtual Agents, a developer must begin by creating a bot, using the dialog box shown in Figure 6-18. This step involves selecting a name, a language, and the environment in which the bot will be created. The process by which Power Virtual Agents creates the account's first bot occurs in the background and can take as long as 15 minutes.

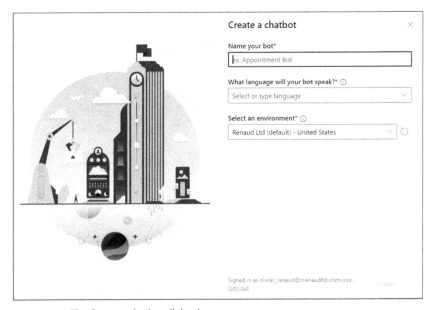

FIGURE 6-18 The Create a chatbot dialog box

To create additional bots, developers must click the Bots panel icon at the upper-right corner of the Power Virtual Agents portal to open the Bots panel shown in Figure 6-19 and then click the +New bot button.

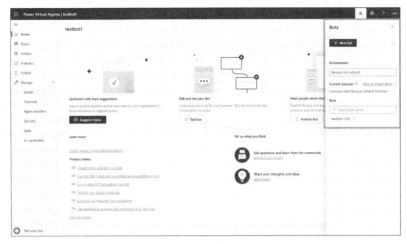

FIGURE 6-19 The Bots panel in the Power Virtual Agents portal

Create a topic

As noted earlier, Power Virtual Agents includes a collection of system topics that covers some of the most common exchanges between bots and customers. When first creating a bot, a developer might want to use the Greeting topic to start the conversation, but after that, developers might have to create topics from scratch to accommodate their business needs.

The prebuilt Greeting topic ends with a message node saying "So, what can I help you with today?" Therefore, the next topic should address the possible responses that the customer might supply to that question. After creating that new topic, the developer can then link it to the Greeting topic to create a conversation by clicking the plus sign and selecting Redirect to another topic, as shown in Figure 6-20.

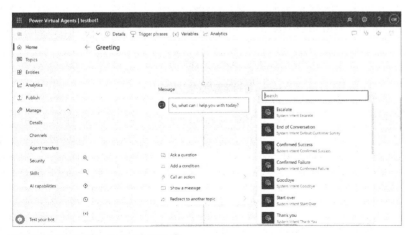

FIGURE 6-20 Linking to another topic

To create a new, blank topic, the developer clicks the +New topic button on the Topics page to open the panel shown in Figure 6-21. The developer can then proceed to create a list of trigger phrases. These phrases should be the most likely responses to the question the bot asks at the end of the Greeting topic.

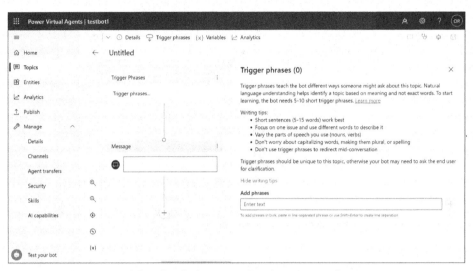

FIGURE 6-21 The +New topic interface in the Power Virtual Agents portal

For this example, *Request* might be an appropriate title, and some possible trigger phrases would be as follows:

- I want to check the status of an order
- I want to return a product
- I want to place an order

Clicking the Details button on the toolbar opens a Details panel in which the developer can specify a name for the topic and, optionally, a display name and a description.

After saving the topic and closing the Details panel, the authoring canvas appears, populated with the supplied trigger phrases and an empty Message node. The developer can add a message or click the plus sign under the Message node to add another node. For example, the developer could select the Ask a question option and use it to provide the customer with three choices, as shown in Figure 6-22.

The Question node allows the developer to branch the conversation by creating three conditions corresponding to the three trigger phrases. The developer can then develop the branch for each option separately to complete the desired task.

FIGURE 6-22 Building a topic in the Power Virtual Agents workspace

Call an action

In the example presented here, the three options presented to the customer might require the bot to do more than just provide prerecorded information. As mentioned earlier in this chapter, Power Virtual Agents can also perform actions by working together with Power Automate. It is actually Power Automate flows that perform actions, but a Power Virtual Agents bot can pass information to a flow and receive information back using variables.

So, for example, if a customer requests the status of an order, the bot can request an order number from the customer and save it to a variable, as shown in Figure 6-23.

FIGURE 6-23 Assigning bot user input to a variable

Launch a Power Automate flow from a chatbot

When the developer clicks the plus sign to add a node and selects Call an action, the option Power Virtual Agents Flow Template appears. This option adds an action to the bot, as shown in Figure 6-24, in which the developer can match up the variables from Power Virtual Agents and Power Automate. This enables the chatbot to pass data to and receive data from the flow, using their respective variables.

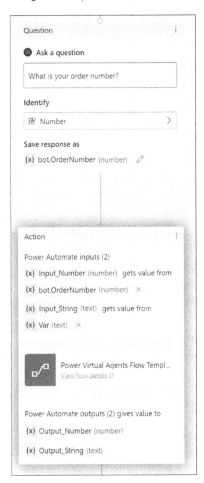

FIGURE 6-24 Matching Power Virtual Agents and Power Automate variables

With the variables matched, the developer can then click the View flow details link to open the Power Automate portal in a separate window and load the Power Virtual Agents Flow Template, as shown in Figure 6-25.

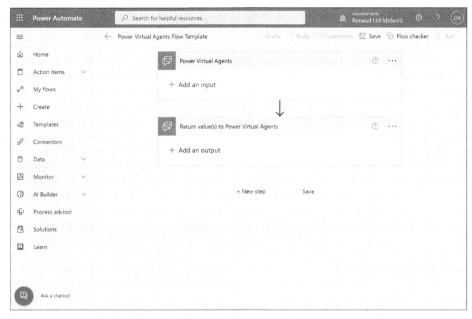

FIGURE 6-25 Power Virtual Agents Flow Template in Power Automate

The developer can then build a flow in Power Automate, as shown in Figure 6-26, using the variable created by the bot to query a database and retrieve the order status. The flow can then pass the order status it has discovered back to the bot using a variable in the same way, and the bot can furnish it to the customer.

FIGURE 6-26 Adding a Power Virtual Agents variable to a Power Automate flow

Publish a chatbot

Once the developer has finished building the conversation for a chatbot, the next steps are to test its functionality and then publish it to create a demonstration website. Once the bot is published, the developer can monitor its use with the Analytics tools provided in the Power Virtual Agents portal.

Testing a bot

In the lower-left corner of the Power Virtual Agents portal is a Test your bot button, which opens a test pane, as shown in Figure 6-27. This pane allows the developer to interact with the bot as a customer while tracking the progress of the conversation through the nodes in the workspace.

FIGURE 6-27 Testing a bot

Acting as a customer, the developer initiates the conversation with one of the topic's trigger phrases. As the test conversation proceeds, each node that is processed appears with a green title bar and a circled check mark in the upper-right corner. If problems occur, the developer can make changes in the workspace and click the Reset button at the top of the pane to begin the conversation again.

Creating a demonstration website

Developers can test their bots as they create them using the testing pane, but to run the bot on an actual website and make it available to customers, the developer must publish it. The Publish page, shown in Figure 6-28, contains a single Publish button that makes the current version of the bot available for distribution to users.

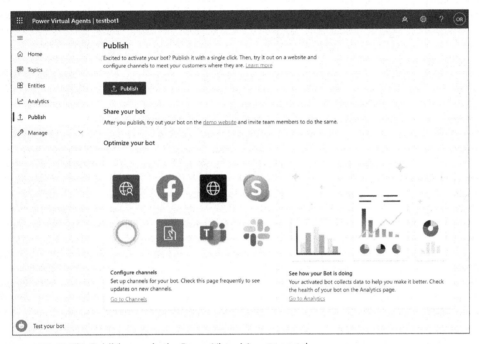

FIGURE 6-28 The Publish page in the Power Virtual Agents portal

Publishing a bot makes it available on a demo website that is fully operational, as shown earlier in this chapter. The demo website is accessible to the internet, but it is not intended to be used as a production platform for the bot.

As mentioned earlier in this chapter, Power Virtual Agents publishes bots to channels, and the demo website has a channel tile of its own, which you can configure by adding a welcome message and suggested trigger phrases, as shown in Figure 6-29.

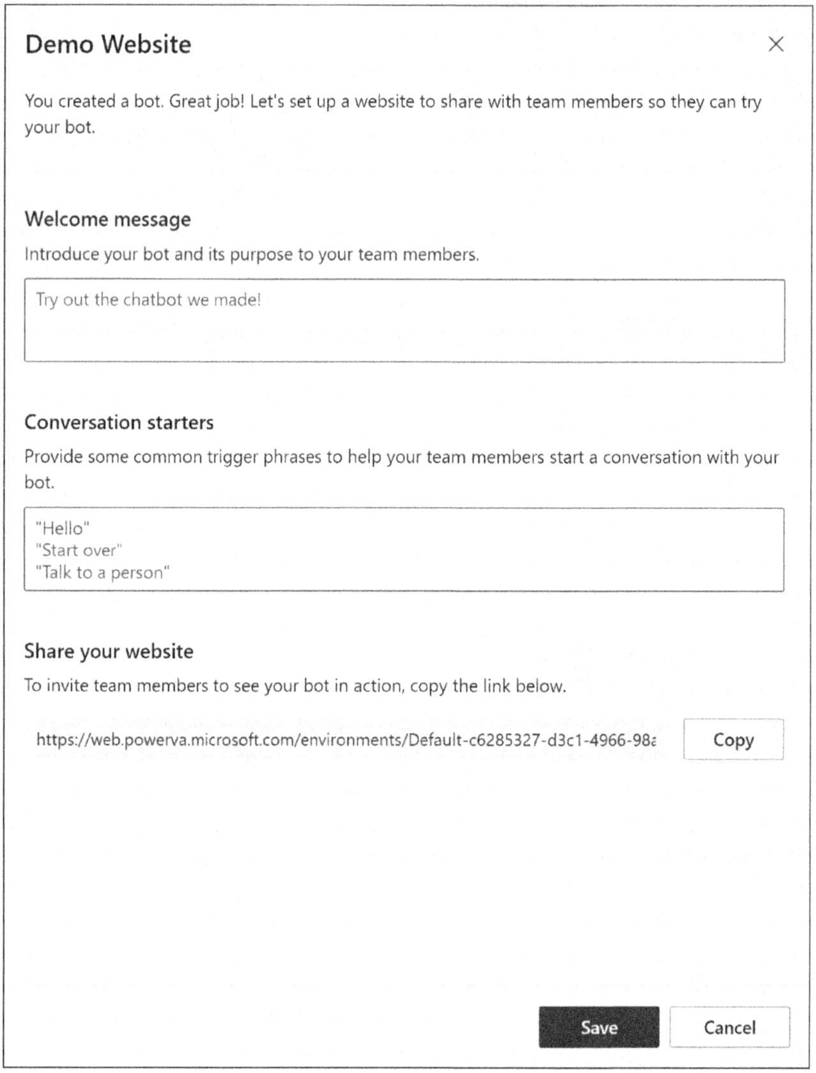

Demo Website   ✕

You created a bot. Great job! Let's set up a website to share with team members so they can try your bot.

Welcome message

Introduce your bot and its purpose to your team members.

> Try out the chatbot we made!

Conversation starters

Provide some common trigger phrases to help your team members start a conversation with your bot.

> "Hello"
> "Start over"
> "Talk to a person"

Share your website

To invite team members to see your bot in action, copy the link below.

https://web.powerva.microsoft.com/environments/Default-c6285327-d3c1-4966-98a   [Copy]

[Save]   [Cancel]

FIGURE 6-29 The Demo Website panel

Publishing a chatbot to the demo website is a simple process that occurs wholly within Power Virtual Agents. To publish a bot to another site on the web, the Custom website channel provides the HTML code needed to embed the bot on a page, as shown in Figure 6-30. Because the embed code calls the bot from the Power Virtual Agents service in the cloud, its content is updated whenever the developer republishes it.

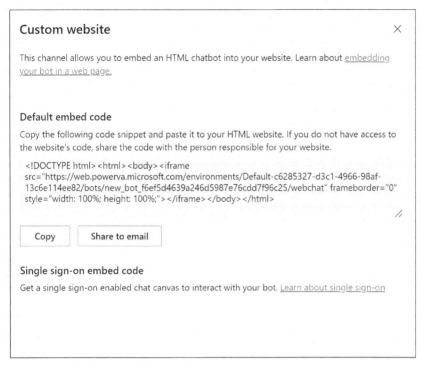

FIGURE 6-30 The Custom website panel

Publishing a bot to other channels can require different procedures, based on the platform with which the developer is working. It might be necessary for the bot developer to work with other administrators within the company to obtain the necessary permissions to add a bot to a platform such as Microsoft Teams or the credentials necessary to manage a company social media account. The tiles for the various channels provide links to instructions for embedding bots in various services, as well as a Bot ID and Tenant ID that uniquely identify the developer's tenancy and the specific bot within that tenancy.

Monitoring chatbot usage

The Analytics page in the Power Virtual Agents portal, shown in Figure 6-31, provides an array of charts that allows developers and administrators to track the number of users that access a bot and examine the results of that usage.

The top row of small area charts provides the following statistics for the range of dates specified in the selector:

- *Total sessions*—Specifies the number of bot sessions that took place
- *Engagement rate*—Specifies the number of bot sessions in which the user's topic was found or the session was escalated
- *Resolution rate*—Specifies the number of bot sessions in which the user responded positively to a customer satisfaction survey

- *Escalation rate*—Specifies the number of bot sessions that were escalated to a human representative

- *Abandon rate*—Specifies the number of bot sessions that were engaged but not resolved or escalated

- *CSAT*—Displays the results of the customer satisfaction survey the bot provides to willing users at the end of the conversation

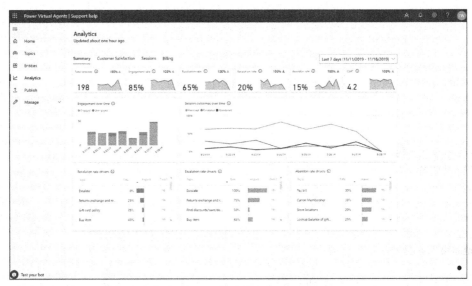

FIGURE 6-31 The Analytics page in the Power Virtual Agents portal

Monitoring chatbot performance

Power Virtual Agents includes a prebuilt End of Conversation topic, shown in Figure 6-32, which includes a survey question that allows users to state whether their session with the bot was successful in answering their questions or solving their problems. This is one way to monitor the performance of a chatbot in terms of customer satisfaction.

The Analytics page includes charts that track the customer survey results generated by the End of Conversation topic, as well as the other possible session outcomes:

- *Engagement*—A session in which the customer supplies a trigger phrase that launches a user-created topic (as opposed to one of the system topics, such as Greeting) or the session ends with the escalation of the issue to a human representative. An engaged session must always be resolved, escalated, or abandoned.

- *Resolution*—An engaged session in which the user responds to the End of Conversation customer satisfaction survey with Yes or with no answer.

- *Escalation*—An engaged session in which the bot transfers the issue to a human representative.

- *Abandonment*—An engaged session that, after one hour elapses, is not resolved or escalated.

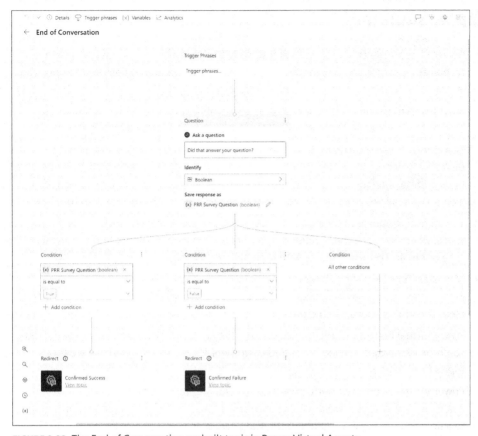

FIGURE 6-32 The End of Conversation prebuilt topic in Power Virtual Agents

Some of the more detailed charts included on the Analytics page are as follows:

- *Session outcomes over time*—A line chart that tracks the daily number of resolved, escalated, and abandoned sessions on separate colored lines.

- *Engagement over time*—A column chart that specifies the daily number of engaged and unengaged sessions.

- *Rate drivers*—Three tables that list the topics with the greatest impact on the bot's resolution, escalation, and abandonment rates. In each table, the Rate figure is the percentage of engaged sessions, including the specified topics that have a Resolved, Escalated, or Abandoned outcome. Impact is a bar representing the resolution, escalation, or abandonment rate of sessions, including the specified topic minus the rate of sessions that do not include the topic. A red bar indicates a greater-than-average resolution, escalation, or abandonment rate; a blue bar indicates a less-than-average rate.

Chapter summary

- Power Virtual Agents is a no-code or low-code tool that allows customer service and technical support personnel themselves to create chatbots and update them as needed.

- Developers can publish chatbots to websites and many other types of platforms, including internal messaging platforms, such as Microsoft Teams, mobile apps, and social media. Power Virtual Agents refers to these places of publication as channels.

- Power Virtual Agents breaks down the conversation between a bot and a user into discrete elements called topics. An entity is a dictionary of terms and phrases that a bot's artificial intelligence uses to identify a concept in a conversation. An action is an element that allows a bot to actually do something beyond conversing with the user.

- The authoring canvas in the Power Virtual Agents portal is the developers' main workspace, where they can specify the trigger phrases that launch the bot and create message nodes and question nodes with branching conditions.

- After starting Power Virtual Agents, a developer must start by creating a bot, which involves selecting a name, a language, and the environment in which the bot will be created. The process occurs in the background and can take as long as 15 minutes.

- Power Virtual Agents includes a collection of system topics that covers some of the most common exchanges between bots and customers. Developers can also create their own topics from scratch.

- Power Virtual Agents can perform actions by working together with Power Automate. It is actually Power Automate flows that perform actions, but a bot can pass information to a flow and receive information back using variables.

- The test pane allows the developer to interact with the bot as a customer while tracking the progress of the conversation through the nodes in the workspace.

- The Publish page contains a single Publish button that makes the current version of the bot available for distribution to users. Developers must republish their bots each time they make changes to them so that the latest version is provided to users.

Thought experiment

In this thought experiment, demonstrate your skills and knowledge of the topics covered in this chapter. You can find answers to this thought experiment in the next section.

Ralph is experimenting with the Power Platform tools, and he has just created a Power Automate flow for his company's technical support department that allows a user to create a new trouble ticket and submit it for attention by the help desk. However, the manager of the tech support department is wary of the help desk being inundated with trouble tickets for trivial issues that the users could conceivably resolve themselves.

Ralph is now looking at the capabilities of Power Virtual Agents, and he wonders if he could use a chatbot to provide users with basic technical support in the form of questions to which they must respond before they are able to fill out a trouble ticket. With the help of the technical support manager, Ralph compiles a list of questions that a help desk representative would ask users when they report some common problems. The questions are phrased so that "No" answers indicate a failure to solve the problem.

Based on this information, answer the following questions:

1. How might Ralph design the chatbot's conversation with the user?

2. How might Ralph incorporate the Power Automate flow he created into the bot's conversation?

Thought experiment answers

This section contains the solution to the thought experiment. Each answer explains why the answer choice is correct.

1. Ralph could create a topic containing a series of Question nodes that attempt to isolate the user's problem. "Yes" responses indicate that the user is experiencing the proposed problem, and the bot could provide information to help the user solve it.

2. After a certain number of "No" responses, indicating that the proposed problems have been ruled out, the conversation should proceed to an Action node that calls the flow in Power Automate and allows the user to fill out and submit a trouble ticket.

Index

Numbers

100% stacked charts, 88

A

AAD (Azure Active Directory)
    authentication, 37
    Power Platform security, 32
abandonment charts, 242
access
    IAM, 32
    Power BI
        access transaction example, 35–36
        accessing data, 108
    Power Platform accessibility guidelines, 50
actions, 72
    calling, 235
    choosing, 76–77
    Compose action, 210
    Create CSV table action, 210–211
    Create HTML table action, 211
    Data Operation actions, 210–212
    deleting rows, 77–78
    dragging/dropping, 210
    Filter array action, 211
    inserting, 209–210
    Join action, 211
    modifying, 208–209
    Parse JSON action, 211–212
    Power Virtual Agents, 226
    Select action, 212
Activity table type, 65
administration
    apps, managing, 41–42
    Microsoft 365, 46–47
    Power Apps, Environment Admin, 38
    Power Platform, 30–32, 46–48
    users
        basic users, 39
        delegates, 39
        managing, 42–44
aggregate functions, 117–118
AI (Artificial Intelligence), Power Virtual Agents, 219–220
AI Builder, 2
alerts, Power BI, 126–127

analytics
    Analytics page, Power Virtual Agents, 242–243
    Power Platform, 54–55
App Designer, Power Apps, 10–12
appending queries, 114
approvals, use cases, 197–198
apps (applications)
    blank apps, data connections, 155–156
    building
        apps, 125
        canvas apps, 152–165
        with Power Apps, 10–12
    Business Central app, 25
    canvas apps, 10, 144–146
        building, 152–165
        connectors, 155–159
        controls, 160–163
        creating from data, 159–160
        data connections, 155–156
        data sources, 153–155, 156–158
        designing the user experience, 160–163
        embedding in Microsoft Teams, 165
        Microsoft Dataverse, 61
        publishing, 163–164
        sharing, 163–164
        templates, 159
    Commerce app, 25
    Customer Service app, 25
    data sources, 153–155
    designing, 10–12
    Dynamic 365 apps
        feedback loops, 24
        list of apps, 24–25
        Power Platform operation, 23–25
    embedding in Microsoft Teams, 165
    Field Service app, 25
    Finance app, 25
    FlooringEstimates app, 160–163
    help desk app, 144–146
    Human Resources app, 25
    licensing, 148
    managing, 41–42
    Marketing app, 25
    Microsoft 365 apps, Power Platform operation, 25–26
    Microsoft Dataverse, storing app data, 60–61
    mobile apps

D

greeting (default), 20
message nodes, 229
question nodes, 230–231, 234
rate drivers charts, 243
resolution charts, 242
session outcomes over time charts, 243
topics, 222–223
    with branching logic, 21
    creating, 233–234
    End of Conversation topic, 242
    linking, 233
trigger phrases, 227–229
triggers, 20
use cases, 218–221
Presentation Role, 35, 36
privacy, Power Platform, 50–52
production environments, 46
proxies, connectors as, 74–75
publishing
    apps, 163–164
    chatbots, 220–221, 238–243
    dashboards, Power BI, 140–141
    desktops, 125
    model-driven apps, 173–174
    reports, 125, 135–136, 140–141
push triggers, 76, 198

Q

queries
    appending, 114
    combining, 114–117
    merging, 114–117
question nodes, 230–231, 234

R

rate drivers charts, 243
real-time workflows, 72
recipients, dashboards, 141
relationships
    many-to-many (N:N) relationships, 68
    many-to-one (N:1) relationships, 68
    peer relationships, 68
    tables, 67–69
removing
    columns, 113–114
    rows, 113–114
renaming elements, 114
Report filters, 128
Report tab, Power BI menu bar, 98
reports
    Audit Reports, STP, 50
    building apps, 125
    Power BI, 6, 101
        creating reports, 132–133
        viewing options, 125

publishing reports, 125, 135–136, 140–141
    sharing reports, 135, 140–141
resolution charts, 242
restricted tables, 66
rows
    deleting, 77–78
    removing, 113–114
run-only users, 40–41

S

Sales app, 24
sandbox environments, 46
scatter charts, 93
scheduled cloud flows, 15–16, 179, 202
security
    IAM, 32
    Microsoft Dataverse, security roles, 39
    Power Apps, 37–39
    Power Automate, 39–41
    Power BI, 32–37, 103–108
    Power Platform
        AAD, 32
        Power Apps, 37–39
        Power Automate, 39–41
        Power BI, 32–37
Select action, 212
service data types, 118–119
services
    Power BI, 99–100
    third-party apps/services, Power Platform consumption of, 29
session outcomes over time charts, 243
Share Dashboard dialog, Power BI, 32–33
shared datasets, use cases, 123–124
sharing
    apps, 38–39, 163–164
    connectors, 82–83
    dashboards, Power BI, 140–141
    flows, Power Automate, 40–41
    model-driven apps, 173–174
    reports, Power BI, 135, 140–141
slicers, Power BI, 128
slow flows, 53
solutions
    creating, 73–74
    managed solutions, 73
    Microsoft Dataverse, 72–74
    unmanaged solutions, 73
stacked charts, 87–88
standard tables, 69–70
storing app data, Microsoft Dataverse, 60–61
STP (Service Trust Portal)
    Audit Reports, 50
    Compliance Manager, 50–51
    Documents & Resources, 50
    Industries & Regions, 50
    Trust Center, 50
subscription interface, Power BI, 126